Designing a Not-for-Profit Compensation System

Designing a Not-for-Profit Compensation System

JoAnn Senger

WILEY

John Wiley & Sons, Inc.

*For my colleagues in diverse not-for-profit organizations
in recognition of their professionalism, hard work,
and continuing service on behalf of the greater good.*

About the Author

JoAnn Senger (Oxnard, CA) is the founder of Senger Services, a consulting firm offering such services as compensation studies, recruitment, policy development, preparation for collective bargaining negotiations, workflow and staffing analysis, security awareness training, and targeted interviewing to a variety of public and not-for-profit organizations. Clients have included: Ventura County; U.S. Navy (through VRMack Management Consultants); Screen Actors Guild; Investigations, Etc.; California Institute of Integral Studies; California Institute of Podiatry; Institute of Transpersonal Psychology; The Fielding Institute; and Western Association of Schools and Colleges (WASC). Senger currently teaches economics for the University of Phoenix and information and cost analysis in HR management for the University of California Santa Barbara's extension program. She has taught benefits and compensation for California Lutheran University's Learning System extension program. Beginning in 2003, she has taught the SHRM preparation course for the SPHR/PHR certification examinations.

Contents

Preface

Like elephants, compensation systems for public and nonprofit organizations may be big, slow to change direction, and exceptionally enduring.

Many readers of this book will have to take that statement on faith because compensation classes and professional association presentations often ignore the existence of the public/nonprofit world. So pervasive is the emphasis on the for-profit environment that the assumption of a direct relationship between operational success, organizational success, and financial success is nearly as invisible as the environment it ignores.

This book will assist in designing and maintaining compensation structures in a public/nonprofit environment rather than serve as a textbook on the various aspects of compensation. The author of this book assumes that readers will have a basic acquaintance with current compensation structures and bases such as overlapping ranges, broadbanding, step structures, commission structures, merit- and competency-based pay, and other aspects of compensation systems.

Professionals in compensation and human resources fields in the public/nonprofit world attend professional events and read professional literature with an automatic translator, factoring in the challenges unique to their organizations and screening out complexities that don't apply. These professionals wrestle with such questions as:

- How is merit defined when good years in the customary business sense (a burst of revenue from successful operations) either cannot exist or cannot be used for compensation purposes?
- How do you structure executive compensation in the absence of stock options?

- Where does the organization obtain bonus money when even exceptionally successful operations may bring in no additional revenue?
- Is "growing the business" even relevant in a public or nonprofit environment and, if relevant, how would one know that the business had grown?

Compensation and human resources professionals may find that the challenges of their environments meet with thinly veiled disdain or worse, amusement. Some professionals imply—or say outright—that the challenges of the public/nonprofit world simply shouldn't exist because able management would meet and eliminate these challenges. Problems so neatly dismissed need not be addressed, and the compensation specialists from the public/nonprofit environment frequently emerge from professional training confused and frustrated, their challenges ignored.

Beginning with definition and ending with reflection, this book seeks to answer the all-important question: *How does one evaluate a compensation technique for relevancy to a specific public or nonprofit environment?* Budget cycles, regulatory constraints, and the roles of boards of directors, to say nothing of the electorate, figure prominently in the public/nonprofit world and may directly or indirectly impact employee compensation at all levels.

No compensation technique, no matter how elegant or ingenious, is worth much if it won't work at home. If compensation specialists in any organization are able to determine what compensation structures are likely to stand the test of time in their home organizations, they will have bridged the gap between theory and practice. This book is intended to help compensation professionals in the public and nonprofit worlds bridge that gap.

METHODOLOGY

In the course of developing this book, I have sought the professional opinions of colleagues in various public and nonprofit environments throughout the United States. Our conversations were structured around a survey (see Appendix A) addressing organizational decisions with respect to compensation, the organizational framework in which the decisions were made, and the compensation structure that resulted from those decisions. Due to the organizationally intimate nature of the survey questions, I have promised strict confidentiality to the participants. The reader can be assured that their views and observations influenced the content of this book in a profound way, and I am most grateful to all those who agreed to donate their time and wisdom to this effort.

In particular, I would like to acknowledge GuideStar's rich resources regarding nonprofit organizations.

JoAnn Senger, MA, SPHR
University of Phoenix Faculty Member

Introduction

If you are reading this book, you are probably contemplating compensation structure issues in an environment often described as "not a company." If so, then this guide is for you.

By introducing a different set of organizational parameters, I hope to make your public/nonprofit environment more intelligible and therefore more rewarding. Most people moving professionally through different environments expect to see changes in organizational priorities. Those who move from the for-profit to the public/nonprofit environment may find organizational priorities so different as to be unrecognizable. Yet, a successful human resources director or compensation manager must be both knowledgeable and comfortable with organizational priorities in order to function effectively.

Those new to the public/nonprofit environment may feel like the expatriate in the following baseball story, struggling to adapt to a foreign way of doing familiar business.

Baseball Story

An employee is sent by his employer to a foreign country on a two-year assignment. He receives a thorough orientation prior to his departure and after six weeks in his new locale, he can say "What time is it?" and maintain a halting business conversation. However, the jokes and easy camaraderie he enjoyed in the past are no longer part of his days.

Looking out the window one day, the expatriate sees his foreign colleagues playing a game on a playing field shaped like a diamond with white squares at each of the points. An individual stands in the middle of the diamond throwing a ball toward another person, who holds a wooden bat. The batter swings the bat, hits the ball, and then runs around the diamond-shaped playing field, stepping on the white squares at each point.

Oh boy, thinks the expatriate. *It's baseball! I used to be pretty good . . . finally, something I can do.*

The expatriate asks to join in and proceeds to hit three home runs over the course of the game. As he runs around the bases he nods to his foreign colleagues who smile graciously but do not cheer, unsurprising in a restrained people. The game ends with the expatriate's team ahead and the expatriate hitting better than anyone else and the star of the day—or so it seems.

After the game, the team manager approaches the expatriate, who is ready to accept congratulations with humility. But that's not what happens. Instead, the manager indicates through the language difficulties that perhaps the expatriate needs more practice. Frustrated and more than a bit confused the expatriate points out that three home runs in one game is an exceptional accomplishment, and after all, their team won.

"No, we lost," says the manager. To the expatriate's amazement, the manager tells him that, in this game, the pitcher is *trying* to hit the bat, the batter *must* swing at every pitch, and low score wins.

It looked like baseball, it played like baseball, but it wasn't *scored* like baseball. Our unfortunate expatriate never inquired about scoring the game, because *he thought he knew.*

Few human resources and compensation specialists want to be in the position of this expatriate, demonstrating technical excellence only to be told that he ran hard and well in the wrong direction. No one wants to hit three home runs in one game and still lose!

What Happens Next?

While step-by-step progression may lack excitement, it never hurts to begin at the beginning and end at the end. This book begins by assessing the nature of the organization, its financial framework, the workforce, and only then examines the jobs and related compensation issues.

Every author must make some assumptions about the reader, and here are mine:

- The reader is inexperienced either in public/nonprofit compensation or in a specific public or nonprofit organization.

- The reader wants to either create or substantially revise a compensation structure for the organization.

- The reader either understands basic compensation principles and techniques or has access to staff that do. Therefore, this book does not go into great detail explaining compensation principles and techniques beyond the basic definitions.

The tie that binds the following chapters together is a series of model Excel spreadsheets, one for each chapter, intended to document the information needed to make compensation structure decisions as well as record the decisions themselves. I have selected spreadsheet examples (MS-Office Excel) instead of word processing examples due to the spreadsheet's calculation capability, its ability to add rows and columns to suit your specific organization, and its capability to print subsets of the information. The reader should be able to build an electronic workbook containing customized spreadsheets based on the samples shown at the end of each chapter.

We will build this workbook one spreadsheet at a time, and you will no doubt want to modify or add rows and/or columns to reflect the reality of your own environment. By way of example, I have named the sample organization "ABC Community Services." Naturally, you will want to substitute your own organization's name and information.

Now, let's get started!

Definitions

This book uses the terms as defined in the following list:

Term	*Definition*
Budget	The timing and periodicity of the organization's revenue stream. For example, a government agency may receive a budget once a year and be required legally to keep expenditures within those limits. Other nonprofit organizations may struggle to estimate revenue and to cope with an unpredictable revenue stream.
Budget process	The activities necessary to raise funds and/or justify a budget request, estimate revenue, and plan expenditures within the budget once it is known; the timeframe and periodicity of the process; and the determination of the amount of funds to be used for salary increases.
Employer	An organization that pays employees on a regular schedule through a payroll process. The organization may or may not use independent contractors or volunteers in addition to employees to accomplish its mission.
Governing body	A board of directors, regents, trustees, the electorate, to name a few.

Term	*Definition*
Job analysis	The process through which the organization analyzes a related set of activities or responsibilities and derives job descriptions and job specifications.
Job evaluation	The technique used by the employer to determine the relative value of jobs:

- *Whole job:* A collection of job content evaluation techniques that compare jobs with each other or against general criteria.

- *Classification plan:* A whole job evaluation technique that places jobs into predetermined categories, or classes, on the basis of class descriptions or benchmark jobs.

- *Point method:* A quantitative job evaluation technique that assigns points to the compensable factors that describe jobs. These points are totaled for each job as an indicator of the overall value of that job. Base pay is then aligned with market rates for benchmark jobs.

- *Factor comparison:* A technique that begins with the selection of benchmark jobs, the selection of compensable factors, and ranking all the benchmark jobs factor by factor.

Nonprofit employer	An employer that may or may not serve its clientele or sell its services for more than the costs involved (i.e., earn a profit). If the employer does earn a profit, that profit is returned to the organization. The organization does not pay income taxes on revenue earned through its primary mission. *Note:* For purposes of this survey, this definition includes both private nonprofit organizations and government agencies.
Pay grade	A pay policy that applies to a group of jobs of similar worth.

Term	*Definition*
Performance management	The process by which an organization communicates to employees what is expected of them, monitors their accomplishments, and responds with appropriate rewards, learning opportunities, and/or corrective actions.
(Bases for) Salary increases	The behavior or job outcome rewarded by the organization through its compensation structure:

- *Merit:* Base pay increase according to a performance evaluation.

- *Seniority:* Base pay increase according to the employee's length of service in the job.

- *Longevity:* Base pay increases awarded to employees who are at their pay grade maximum and not likely to move into higher pay grades.

- *Incentive (or variable) pay:* Compensation, other than base wages or salaries, that fluctuate according to the attainment of some standard, for example, a preestablished formula such as a commission plan, individual or group goals, or organization-wide revenue.

- *Person-based pay:* Increase in base pay because the employee acquires additional skills (physical worker), knowledge (professional worker), or competencies (manager).

CHAPTER 1

Organization—Who Are We?

A simple enough question, and if the organization is large or well-known, a compensation manager may feel that the question is unnecessary. However, current human resources (HR) professional training literature, such as the Society for Human Resource Management (SHRM) certification preparation materials, indicates that successful HR policies and practices must be harmonious with the nature of the organization and its strategy to effectively support its mission. *Nothing is more worthy of close analysis than the organization itself.*

The first spreadsheet in the series (ORG) is the shortest, but the information to be recorded there may strongly influence, if not determine, all that is to come (see Spreadsheet 1 at the end of this chapter, as well as in Appendix B). We will begin with the most obvious yet most misunderstood descriptor: Type of Organization.

TYPE OF ORGANIZATION

This field is intended to provide the briefest description of the organization: government (public) or nonprofit (private). Most of my professional colleagues work in the for-profit world, and their opinions vary widely as to the definition of those organizations that "don't have to make a profit."

Some misconceptions that have reached me include the following:

- All private employers are for-profit.
- Nonprofit means government.
- Nonprofit means that the organization can't make a profit.

To add to the confusion, some terms used in the media mix the terminology with such phrases as "public companies" (meaning for-profit, publicly traded companies) and "privately held companies" (companies whose stock is not publicly traded) to say nothing of "public utilities" such as those public utilities that are privately owned, may be publicly traded, and are subject to close regulatory scrutiny.

In this book, the public sector includes government at all levels and may include related organizations such as state universities and other educational institutions often not considered part of government. Nonprofit organizations are private, self-governing, overseen by volunteers, do not distribute any profits to the owners (there are no owners), and meet the 501(c)(3) standards set by the Internal Revenue Service (IRS). Religious institutions, some healthcare organizations, professional associations themselves, historic preservation societies, art and cultural groups, and many other organizations fall into this category.[1] In common speech, the term "private sector" usually means the for-profit sector of the economy. However, nonprofit organizations are considered private. As Hutton and Phillips point out, nonprofit organizations are formed to benefit the public, or a particular subset of the public, but not one person or one family.[2]

The reader might well ask why this book addresses two such different types of organizations: public and nonprofit. The answer is simple: I am putting these two types of organizations into one book because my human resources colleagues seem to view them as more similar than different. Why? Because these organizations "don't have to make a profit."

At this point, the compensation manager need only determine whether the organization is a government agency or related entity (established, monitored, and/or supported primarily by the general public), or a nonprofit organization as formally defined by the Internal Revenue Service.

OPERATIONAL FOCUS

The compensation manager will probably have no difficulty describing the organization's operational focus. A government agency might focus on law enforcement, highway construction and maintenance, the judicial system, agricultural support and inspections, healthcare, or libraries, to name a few. The formal nonprofit organizations can be religious institutions, charities, zoos or animal sanctuaries, libraries and foundations, as well as other entities. A nonprofit school of dentistry might provide instruction to future dentists and, as part of that instructional mission, run dental clinics for the underprivileged, the elderly, and students.

MISSION STATEMENT

The public/nonprofit organizations are bound by their missions. Police departments cannot diversify into weapons manufacture; churches cannot establish a Sunday activity to hire employees, sell tax accounting services, and bring in extra cash above and beyond the cost of the services provided in order to pay the church elders bonuses. Public schools cannot design, make, and sell a new line of school uniforms for a profit. At least, these organizations cannot do these things and remain congruent with the public trust and IRS regulations.

For-profit organizations may diversify, acquire other companies or be acquired, change mission, change locations, and make other profound changes. The public or nonprofit organization can also make changes but the range of possibilities is more limited. A county government does not usually acquire or merge with another county government; churches normally do not affiliate with another religion in order to broaden their donations base. *The public/nonprofit world is usually more stable in its focus and stays centered in its mission.*

In our sample organization, ABC Community Services, the only descriptive information displayed on every spreadsheet is the mission statement. A compensation manager should be able to obtain the mission statement from the organization with ease. If not, it is crucial to find out why.

NUMBER OF YEARS IN EXISTENCE

Your organization's history is another piece of information that should be readily available. Public and nonprofit organizations typically have greater job stability. You may have several colleagues who have sufficient seniority to know or even remember the early history of your organization. Knowing how the organization got where it is today will serve you well.

GEOGRAPHICAL PRESENCE

Is your organization physically located on only one site, multiple sites within a city, within multiple cities, multiple states, or even in more than one country? This information, too, should be readily available. If there are multiple sites, you should know where the headquarters is located and where the governing body meets. If fortunate, you may be located at the organizational headquarters. If not so fortunate, you will want to visit the organization's headquarters and establish solid professional relations with peers and superiors.

DESCRIPTION OF OPERATIONS

The information on this row on the spreadsheet should describe the organization's operations as concisely as possible. Such descriptions include but are not limited to:

- Nature of clientele
- Physical, mental, or emotional caregiving to clients
- Any physical operations such as the delivery or preparation of such items as clothes or food to various locations according to a schedule
- Regular public events such as religious services or school hours
- Hours of operation (especially 24/7)
- Physical risks to employees, for example, law enforcement, fire protection
- Degree of education or certification required in order to provide services, for example, Ph.D. or equivalent, RN license

- Type of services provided, for example, tax collection, education, postal service

Record the answers on the ORG Spreadsheet (Spreadsheet 1).

NOTES

1. *Nonprofit Kit for Dummies,* Stan Hutton and Frances Phillips, 2001, Hoboken, NJ: John Wiley & Sons, pp. 8–17.
2. Ibid., p. 20.

SPREADSHEET 1   ABC COMMUNITY SERVICES—
THE ORGANIZATION

Note: The mission statement is the most important piece of information on this worksheet and appears in the heading on all subsequent worksheets.

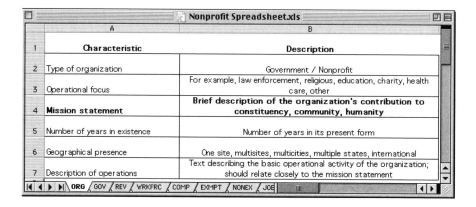

	A	B
	Characteristic	Description
1		
2	Type of organization	Government / Nonprofit
3	Operational focus	For example, law enforcement, religious, education, charity, health care, other
4	**Mission statement**	**Brief description of the organization's contribution to constituency, community, humanity**
5	Number of years in existence	Number of years in its present form
6	Geographical presence	One site, multisites, multicities, multiple states, international
7	Description of operations	Text describing the basic operational activity of the organization; should relate closely to the mission statement

Nonprofit Spreadsheet.xls

ORG / GOV / REV / WRKFRC / COMP / EXMPT / NONEX / JOB

CHAPTER 2

Governance—Who's in Charge?

The human resources department is normally in charge of the care and feeding of the organization chart, a series of boxes and lines representing the organization's formal lines of authority. Usually presented in crisp black and white, the organization chart is—or should be—a monument to logic and the hierarchical structure. However, there may be a good deal more to the story of the organization than suggested by the lines of formal authority. Informal authority, the power of personality, influence beyond the bounds of job, special arrangements, and many other factors not shown on the organization chart influence what gets done, when it gets done, and how it gets done.

The formal authority structure in a public or nonprofit environment is less obvious to the new employee and possibly more diffuse. There may be multiple authorities with legitimately separate agendas and some subunits that are almost autonomous or can act autonomously without fear of interference.

This chapter looks at the role of the organization's governing body and how its workings might impact a compensation manager trying to establish or make substantial major changes to the organization's compensation structure. Information about your organization may be recorded on the second spreadsheet, GOV. If other characteristics occur to you, then the spreadsheet can be expanded with respect to both rows and columns to accommodate the unique aspects of your organization. For example, a religious organization might require that at least half of the board of directors be ordained, and that all ordained board members must be present for a quorum.

GOVERNING BOARD

Public agencies are typically run by either an elected or appointed individual or group of individuals. These individuals serve at the pleasure of the electorate or the person who holds the job with the power to appoint. For example, a board of governors, appointed by the president of the United States, runs the United States Postal Service. These individuals serve for life or until a president of the United States "unappoints" them.

Nonprofit organizations have a board composed of men and women serving as directors, trustees, regents, or some similar term. These men and women serve without compensation and actually do direct these nonprofit organizations. The *employees* of the organization from the most senior manager, such as the executive director, to the lowest level employee hold jobs designed to fulfill the mission according to the strategies and goals set by the board of directors. In that respect, one might say that the chief executive officer (CEO) of the nonprofit organization drives the train on a track and at a speed determined by the governing board.

The compensation manager charged with making substantial changes or even designing a new compensation structure must become familiar with every possible detail about the workings of this governing body. At the risk of stating the obvious, the first detail is to know and scrupulously use *the exact name* chosen by your organization for its governing board, for example, board of directors, board of trustees, board of regents, or board of supervisors.

If your function, location, or some accident of fate places you in close proximity to one or more board members, you may be in a unique position to obtain a strategic organizational perspective directly applicable to the design and maintenance of a new or substantially revised compensation structure. The advantages and disadvantages of contact with board members could include:

ADVANTAGES

- Opportunity to informally talk about organizational strategies and goals
- Opportunity to present compensation structure ideas to someone whose opinion carries weight

- Opportunity to get feedback from someone who will quickly spot any mismatches between your approach and basic organizational characteristics
- Advance knowledge of shifts in organizational priorities

DISADVANTAGES

- Board members may treat you like their own staff
- Board members may bypass your boss and speak to you directly, thereby causing tension between you and your boss
- You may become involved, unwillingly, in power struggles between various board member factions
- You may lose sight of the fact that you need to get along with all board members

Number of Members

The larger your governing board, the more administrative overhead is involved in preparing for and following up on board meetings. If your boss must bear the burden of this administrative overhead, then you may share in that burden as well.

The number of board members determines the number required for a quorum, the minimum number of members required to be present in order to vote on an issue. *If your compensation implementation effort requires a board vote, then the number of "yes" votes and the number in a quorum could be of critical importance.*

Some boards may be large enough to appoint either standing or ad hoc subcommittees. If there is a subcommittee charged with compensation matters, especially with your specific project, acquainting yourself with subcommittee members and subcommittee proceedings will be of the highest priority.

Board Member Finances

Do the board members receive any kind of financial assistance, such as travel and other expenses, country club memberships, or any other remuneration?

If so, the compensation manager will need to know the circumstances under which the funds are given and received. If the governing board members are appointed or elected officials and receive a salary, that salary amount may act as a cast-iron ceiling on any salary structure you may devise for other employees.

ELECTED/APPOINTED OFFICIALS

If your organization is run by elected/appointed officials, the compensation manager should know how elections are handled, who can appoint and "unappoint" these officials, and whether the electorate can recall any or all of them. These events are beyond the compensation manager's control or influence, and a compensation structure project can get lost in election preparations or a debate over a hotly contested appointment.

BOARD MEMBER TITLES

The compensation manager should maintain a current list of all board member titles. These titles may impact or influence the titles permitted in the organization and their relative significance in the hierarchy.

EX OFFICIO BOARD MEMBERS

The compensation manager needs to know how many board members serve ex officio (by virtue of their title) and whether these members have a vote or may be counted in a quorum. A nonvoting board member, or one unable to attend board meetings regularly, cannot effectively support a new compensation structure requiring board approval other than to exercise influence with other board members. That influence, of course, could be considerable.

TERMS OF SERVICE

Designing, implementing, and maintaining a compensation structure is demanding enough in the best of circumstances. If the board members serve a sufficiently predictable length of time and if the terms served are staggered (meaning that only some board members come up for renewal at any one time), then there will be more stability of direction. The compensation manager may want to carefully time any required governing board action on the new or revised compensation structure to a period of time when the board is not distracted by possible changes in membership.

Quorum for Decisions

The compensation manager should know how many board members out of the total number of members must be present to vote on an organizational matter and which members are critical. For example, the board may be unable to act unless 60 percent of the members *and* the chairperson are present. The incapacity or death of one or more board members could postpone action on the compensation structure proposal, requiring a different approach to implementation.

Further, is there a way for the board to give interim approval to a project? If so, has such approval ever been given? How was such interim approval obtained?

Number of Meetings per Year

If the board must vote affirmatively in order to allow the compensation manager to address specifics or implement the new/revised compensation structure, then the compensation manager needs to know how often and when the board meets in a given year. Does the board meet every month? Are each of these meetings action meetings, that is, meetings in which the board votes on one or more issues placed before it? Or, are one or more meetings devoted to special efforts such as strategic planning? The timing of action meetings could become of great importance to the compensation manager's implementation efforts.

Role of the Governing Body

Spreadsheet 2 at the end of this chapter (GOV) lists several issues that might be addressed by a board of directors. (This spreadsheet is also shown in Appendix B.) These areas include fundraising; budget request and negotiation; approval of compensation matters such as the salary increase budget; changes to the compensation structure or specific salaries; and the approval of new hires for one or more jobs. If these and any other roles fall into the purview of the governing board, the new/revised compensation structure will have to accommodate the governing board's role.

The more you know about your governing board, the more successful your planning and implementation efforts are likely to be.

Mission Statement: Provide Service to Those in Need

	A	B
	Nonprofit Spreadsheet.xls	
1	Governance	
2	Governing board	Name
3	Number of members	#
4	Board member finances	Y/N
5	Elected/Appointed officials	Y/N
6	Board member titles	List
7	Ex officio members:	
8	Number:	
9	Titles:	
10	Terms of service	Number of years, staggered terms (Y/N)
11	Quorum for decisions	Required attendance (percent/number/specific board members)
12	Number of meetings per year	Number and schedule
13	Role of governing body:	
14	Conduct fundraising	Y/N
15	Conduct budget request and negotiations	Y/N
16	Approve salary increase budget	Y/N
17	Approve changes to compensation structure	Y/N
18	Approve CEO/Executive director salary	Y/N
19	Approve top management salaries	Y/N
20	Approve other salaries	Y/N
21	Approve (some) new hires	Y/N
22	Other	Describe

ORG **GOV** REV WRKFRC COMP EXMPT NONEX JOE

CHAPTER 3

Revenue—Where Do We Get Our Money?

It's been many years since a senior systems analyst, three months into a new job, asked the project leader that question. I was that systems analyst. Our project team was exploring the possibility of sharing library resources among three dissimilar higher education institutions: a private research university, a public research university, and a technical institute.

Before the days of online registration, students had to go to the main library to obtain their library cards. As an employee new to the public/nonprofit world, I saw the students lined up outside the library and thought, *"Ah, revenue. Look at all these customers."* Doing some quick calculations in my head, I ascertained that revenue from the "sale" of library cards was catastrophically inadequate to keep the library open, much less buy and process additional library materials. Then, with a force still remembered today, my thoughts stumbled across an apparent fiscal contradiction: *How can the library get sufficient revenue from these students when the money from all these library cards wouldn't support the library for a day?*

So I did ask the project leader the question "Where we do get our money?" and received an incomprehensible reply: "Oh, you want to know about the budget." No, I had no interest in "the budget." How could we possibly do a budget when we didn't know where the money came from, or how much we had? The budget could wait; I was interested in *revenue*.

Ten years later at another higher education institution, I acquired a basic understanding of the relationship between budget and revenue in the public and nonprofit worlds. This chapter is intended to share that understanding and its ramifications with you. In a nutshell, budget and revenue are two words that are used indistinguishably in most public and nonprofit organizations.

In the for-profit world, organizations provide goods and services to the market for a price. If customers buy these goods and services, the organizations get to keep the money resulting from the sales. This money is called *revenue* and is normally considered to be earned and owned by the organization. Out of this revenue, the for-profit organizations pay the expenses incurred while producing the goods and services (including the cost of employees), and the organization keeps the money left over.

This leftover money is commonly called profit, and for-profit organizations want this amount to be as large as possible. They may use this money for whatever purposes they choose, staying within applicable laws and regulations. When there are more customers than usual, under normal circumstances, profits are bigger than usual. (Note that this very simple business model ignores the complications of income taxes, paying off loans, and other business financial demands.)

For-profit organizations typically call this incoming stream of money such names as "revenue," "gross income," or "sales." These organizations track incoming and outgoing money through accounting systems and periodically provide governmental authorities and possibly the investment community with reports about the magnitude of the money coming in and the money going out. Interested parties analyze these reports for a variety of purposes including determination of tax obligations and investment desirability.

The public or nonprofit organization typically begins its fiscal year knowing, or estimating, its revenue for the coming year. Management may estimate the magnitude of this incoming money or negotiate with external agencies for the money. Once the amount is estimated or negotiated, the organization will act as if the incoming money is real and then plan, or *budget,* accordingly. Put simply, the organization acts as if the budget *is* the revenue. At the beginning of the fiscal year, the organization knows how much money will be available—or will be assumed to be available—to fund its operations. Operational success may have little or no effect on that amount of revenue in that year, or in the foreseeable future.

Public and nonprofit organizations receive favorable tax treatment on the basis of either the public trust or in pursuance of a mission and the establishment of an organizational structure determined suitable for nonprofit (and therefore nontaxable) status. The burden of proof rests on the public/nonprofit organization to display how funds received into the organization are used in conformity with the intentions of the fund providers. These funds and any resulting leftover money belong to the organization (what would otherwise be called *profit*) and can only be spent in the furtherance of its mission.

In public and nonprofit organizations, the incoming stream of money is usually called *funding,* and funds typically arrive with strings attached. The concept of "earning" money does not apply in quite the same way although the public/nonprofit world provides goods and services. For example, a charity may provide goods and services such as food, clothing, shelter, and healthcare to the homeless. However, the provision of these goods and services results in expenses but no revenue because the homeless cannot pay for them. So, where does the revenue come from? Charities typically rely heavily on donations: gifts of money from individuals who do not themselves need or want the goods or services provided by the organization. In this case, the operational focus (facilities for the homeless) is separate from the revenue focus, which targets donations made by individuals who, by definition, are not direct customers or clients.

When a government agency awards a research grant to a university, one might say that the agency is purchasing a service, that is, research, and will receive a full report on the methodology, the experiment, and any results of the research effort. But that is not enough. In addition, the granting government agency expects to receive periodic reports showing how the funds were used including any equipment or supplies purchased with the funds, the job titles of any employees paid with these funds, and the circumstances and amount of time spent by these employees while being paid from these funds.

Even though the university provides the research services in return for money received, the frame of reference is other than buy-and-sell. Instead, the granting agency is supporting the university in its efforts to fulfill its own research mission. The funds provided by the granting agency may be tax dollars given to the granting agency through the public trust. Therefore, the agency has a duty to its own fund providers, the taxpayers, to verify that such funds are expended in the public interest. The university, unlike a private company, cannot simply use the money as it sees fit and let the results stand on their own. Instead, the university must spend the grant money according to certain rules and then go on record as having done so.

Nonprofit organizations must serve a double bottom line: to manage money in a responsible manner (which may include generating a surplus) and to enhance the well-being of the public they are dedicated to serve. This two-sided success criterion impacts compensation so that surplus earnings may not be distributed to employees, the executive director, or board members at the end of the year. While employees are entitled to receive reasonable compensation as indicated by the external labor market and the organization's size, the organization must be careful to avoid any appearance of "profit-sharing." Reasonable compensation is one of the requirements of operating in accordance with the public trust.

FUND SOURCES

The implications of this funding versus operations dichotomy on a new or revised compensation structure will become clearer as you become more familiar with your public or nonprofit organization. *At this point, a compensation manager should obtain fund source information from the last complete fiscal year showing all fund sources for that year, the respective dollar amounts for each fund source, and the percent of the total funding represented by each fund source.* It is important to know where the incoming money originates, the respective amounts, and the respective rankings of major to minor fund sources (see Spreadsheet 3 (REV) at the end of this chapter and in Appendix B).

ANNUAL BUDGET CYCLE

The compensation manager should meet with budget managers, accountants, and others who can provide an annual timeline for the preparation of the budget for the coming fiscal year. Once the budget for the coming year is known, when is the budget available to be spent by the organization? How does the compensation manager find out what the budget will be and what portion of the budget will be available for compensation and related expenses, including salary increases? Who has the formal authority to communicate the details of the coming year's budget?

The relationship between the fiscal year, the calendar year, and the operational year can be complex with several different timelines. For example, educational institutions often follow a July 1–June 30 fiscal year, produce various financial documents on a calendar year basis (such as W-2s), but actually operate on an academic year that begins in September and ends in May.

The answers to these questions and the timing of the budget process will determine, in part, when the compensation manager presents the proposal for the new or revised compensation structure and, to some extent, how and when that structure is implemented.

FORMAL BUDGET REQUEST PROCESS

If there are budget request(s) to be prepared, the compensation manager needs to know when such requests must be submitted and to whom, what information is contained within each budget request, and when the result of the budget request effort will be known. Is the budget determined, in whole or in part, by external agencies? Is the compensation manager expected to make a formal report each year concerning the funds needed for compensation-related matters in the coming budget year? Who internally approves the request or the budget for the coming year?

Typically, the budget request process, whether determined externally by funding agencies or internally through budget and other managers, or both, ends with a determination of the funds available for all purposes, not just compensation-related matters. The compensation manager will want to know whether there is any flexibility in the budget for new hires, bonuses, or other special compensation needs, or whether an amount must be built into the budget. If possible, the compensation manager will want to be a part of the process, and this participation rests on a complete understanding of the process as it relates to compensation.

REQUIRED REPORTING

Public and nonprofit organizations receiving government funds will probably be informed as to the reporting requirements entailed in receiving such funds. The organization cannot simply use the money as it wishes within budget constraints.

Government reports can be quite extensive and detailed, and the organization may employ one or more people who make such reporting their major or sole activity. These employees may be in continuous communication with various government agencies throughout the year. If compensation is one of the areas to be reported—a common enough requirement—then the compensation manager may be charged with oversight of the reporting process or even with report generation itself. If so, this will be a major activity with deadlines to be respected.

Other fund sources may require reports on activities, or the organization may decide that some reports would be prudent, whether required or not. The professionalism of the reports is an important face the organization presents to the external world. The online resource GuideStar provides information about various nonprofit organizations including their financial profiles.

FUND ACCOUNTING

Your organization may have a formal accounting approach that tracks every dollar coming into the organization according to its source until it leaves the organization. If such an accounting system is used in your organization, you must to understand the accounts and their related coding structure.

Fund sources may be described as:

- *Unrestricted*—to be spent however the organization wishes.
- *Permanently restricted*—to be retained as principal and may be invested but not spent.
- *Temporarily restricted*—the income or interest from permanently restricted funds. These temporarily restricted funds may be used only for certain purposes or at certain times.

FUNDRAISING

For those organizations permitted to seek funding from the general public, fundraising can become an extremely important function resulting in a major portion of the organization's finances. The compensation manager will want to know if:

- Fundraising is a routine activity.
- Fundraising is (also) done on an ad hoc basis.
- The compensation manager is expected to be involved in fundraising.
- Some of the funds are constrained and cannot—or must—be used for compensation-related matters.

The compensation manager will want to know how the budget for the coming year addresses donations. Is the budget for the coming year built on the assumption that future donations will be at least as much as the current year, the average of the previous five years, or an amount determined by some other algorithm?

If donations were to be greater than usual in any particular year, could the extra money beyond budget be used for compensation purposes? In other words, is it possible for the organization to have "a good year" and share the wealth with employees? Or, would that be contrary to the regulations governing the organization, or to the internal or external political climate, or to a controlling ideology?

DONORS

The compensation manager will want to know if any donors have a *de facto* influence over any organizational operations, even if they are not on the governing board. Are any major donors experts in human resources-related functions and available for consultation? Would it be prudent—or counter-productive—to include such donors in the compensation manager's efforts?

Does the organization maintain a donor database, sponsor routine mailings, social activities, or other activities that target donors? Is there a formal development office charged with bringing in donations? If so, how will this office expect to be compensated, and will the development office's expectations mesh comfortably with donor expectations regarding compensation levels and the use of their donations? Are any donors vehemently opposed to the use of their contributions for overhead?

GOVERNMENT SUPPORT

Is the organization a public agency, supported in whole or in part by the taxpaying population? If so, what is the role of the electorate? What is the role of the local legislature, especially with respect to compensation? Is there a civil service-type structure, or an expectation of conformity with such a structure?

Government funding usually means government influence and possibly even control. If the compensation manager's new or revised compensation structure must be in conformity with a government structure or will be heavily influenced by such a structure, it is best to know this at the outset.

BUDGET BASED ON REVENUE PREDICTIONS

Your organization may experience the budget as the amount of money that may be spent in the current year regardless of how well the organization performs its mission, whatever abundance the general economy may bestow on other economic sectors, or even what unexpected gifts or special funds may come into the organization. Under such circumstances, the budget takes on a cast-iron quality, a bottom line unto itself. The compensation manager should have an idea of how budget/revenue predictions for the coming year are made and who makes them, whether internal experts or external legislative bodies, or both. Your organization's budget may be tied to any number of external realities beyond your control.

Further, the compensation manager should be aware of any unspoken algorithms that could place limits on the compensation structure. In Chapter 2, "Governance—Who's in Charge?" (*Board Member Finances*), the salaries of the governing board place an absolute limit on the salaries that could be paid to any other employee in the organization. Other organizations may have similar expectations regarding salary increase budgets as well and look to the external labor market, to salary increases in another organization, or even to the Consumer Price Index as a guide or limit on internal salary increases.

VOTER INFLUENCE

The role of the electorate may be key or tangential to the organization's operations and revenue stream. The compensation manager should ascertain how the electorate could possibly affect the organization's revenue, especially that portion reserved for compensation.

SPREADSHEET 3   ABC COMMUNITY SERVICES—
REVENUE

Mission Statement: Provide Service to Those in Need

	A	B
		Nonprofit Spreadsheet.xls
1	Fund sources	List names, amounts, and percents
2	Annual budget cycle	Y/N - describe
3	Formal budget request process	Y/N - describe
4	Required reporting:	Y/N - describe
5	Government contracts	Y/N - describe
6	Other required reporting	Y/N - describe
7	Fund accounting	Y/N - describe
8	Fundraising	Y/N - describe
9	Donors	Y/N - describe
10	Government support	Y/N - describe
11	Budget based on revenue predictions	Y/N - describe
12	Voter influence	Y/N - describe

ORG / GOV / **REV** / WRKFRC / COMP / EXMPT / NONEX / JOB

Legend:

Fund Sources: List each fund source in the previous fiscal year with each respective total annual dollar amount and percentage of total funding.

Annual Budget Cycle: The timing of budget activity, lines of authority for approvals, degree of detail.

Formal Budget Request Process: Is there a formal or informal process through which the organization obtains its budget for the coming fiscal year? If so, describe its timeframe, administrative burden, and other aspects.

Required Reporting: Does the organization have to file reports for government(s) based on the type(s) of funding it receives? If so, what types of reports, how often, and degree of administrative burden? Does the organization have to file reports to nongovernment entities based on the type(s) of funding it receives? If so, what types of reports, how often, and degree of administrative burden?

Fund Accounting: Does the organization use this type of accounting to track the use of each dollar of funding received into the organization?

Legend (continued):

Fundraising: A formal or informal and coordinated effort, routine or ad hoc, to persuade individuals outside the organization to donate funds. Describe the administrative burden, percent of budget obtained through this process, and any other aspects of fundraising.

Donors: Individuals outside the organization who have donated funds to it, currently or in the past, or might donate in the future. There may be significant administrative activity around these individuals.

Government Support: What sort of governmental influence impacts the organization including funding, regulatory control, budget approval, voter influence, or other?

Budget Based on Revenue Predictions: What are the predictive methods and algorithms used to forecast the budget for the coming year? Is revenue considered fixed or can the budget vary throughout the year?

Voter Influence: How can voters impact the organization?

CHAPTER 4

Workforce—Who Are These People?

$\mathbf{A}$ny new employee is bound to take great interest in his or her new colleagues, the population of fellow workers. New compensation managers should be no exception. The organization already has a workforce, and that workforce receives pay on a regular basis. Therefore, a de facto compensation structure already exists, and the workforce knows that structure as the status quo. You, the compensation manager, are working to change that status quo.

The compensation manager needs some basic demographic information about these new colleagues, the existing workforce. These basic demographic statistics include a preliminary division of the workforce into the current employee groups. The fourth spreadsheet (WRKFRC) is intended to contain basic workforce information, a preliminary sketch based on workforce population and job characteristics (see Spreadsheet 4 at the end of this chapter and in Appendix B).

EMPLOYEE GROUP

The workforce can be divided into various groups according to the characteristics of the jobs and the workforce demographics. The initial division of the workforce is based on a comparison of the nature of the work against the provisions of the Fair Labor Standards Act. That evaluation will designate some jobs as *exempt* (exempt from FLSA overtime provisions) and others as *nonexempt* (eligible for overtime). Spreadsheet 4, the WRKFRC spreadsheet, displays some additional suggested employee groups further subdividing these two broad exempt and nonexempt groupings.

Your organization's employee groups may differ greatly from those shown on Spreadsheet 4, although the exempt/nonexempt categories will almost certainly apply. A compensation manager should display sensitivity to the terminology used to name these employee groups. Certain terms may be acceptable as well as commonly understood, while other terms may have a history so negative as to compromise the viability of any new or revised compensation structure. A compensation manager should not hesitate to further refine or even substantially change these employee groups in order to provide a workable frame of reference for the new or revised compensation system.

MALE/FEMALE

Dividing each employee group into male and female subcategories may expose workforce patterns that could prove troublesome, even discriminatory. Any such troublesome patterns may need to be addressed in the new or significantly revised structure. If this basic demographic information exposes practices that systematically disadvantage one gender or the other, the compensation manager may wish to further subdivide the workforce into equal employment opportunity (EEO) reporting categories. EEO reporting is probably a requirement for your organization in any case, and knowing whether your organization is vulnerable on EEO issues enables you to factor in the kind of controls and monitoring necessary to show good faith efforts to achieve sufficient diversity and fair human resources practices throughout the workforce.

EEO complaints may be made on any basis in the following list:

- Race and color—Black
- Race and color—White
- Race and color—American Indian/Alaskan Native
- Race and color—Asian/Pacific Island
- Religion
- National origin—Hispanic

- National origin—Other
- Age
- Gender—female
- Disability—mental
- Gender—male
- Disability—physical
- Reprisal

FULL-TIME, PART-TIME, AND VARIABLE-TIME APPOINTMENTS

Although some organizations may employ only full-time employees, other organizations employ workers under a variety of part-time arrangements. In addition, an organization may use the variable-time appointment in which the employee works a minimum amount of time and, as needed and by agreement, may work more. Or conversely, the employee may normally work full-time but be assured only of a lesser percentage of time. Variable-time appointments can give organizations a very quick budget reduction potential through reductions in time, a mechanism less disruptive to the workforce than a layoff.

APPOINTMENT TERMS

Each employee group may contain employees working under such arrangements as employment at will, an employment contract, tenure or tenure track appointment, collective bargaining contract, or some other arrangement. This information could bring to the surface potentially discriminatory practices if men and women, or various EEO categories previously cited, systematically work under different terms of appointment while belonging to the same employee group and possibly doing similar work. Systematic differences are particularly troubling if the differing terms of appointment consistently advantage one group over another.

The compensation manager will also want to find out why the organization uses the current appointment arrangements. Reasons for the current practices might be no more than historic accident or, more purposely, the result of a formal legal opinion by the organization's legal counsel.

Whatever the reasons are, they may impose certain constraints on the future compensation structure.

UNIONIZED

Some or all of the employees in the nonexempt employee groups may be represented by labor unions. If there are multiple unions, the compensation manager will want to subdivide the employee groups accordingly. In addition, some exempt groups may be involved in professional associations or some other collective organizations that strongly influence the terms and conditions of appointment for those in that employee group. If so, the compensation manager might want to record the existence of such a near-representative organization.

AVERAGE YEARS OF SERVICE

This statistic shows the average years of service with the organization for the employees in that employee group, men and women separately and across EEO categories if you have chosen to add them. This information indicates the maturity of the workforce, the level of employment stability in the organization, and may point to other aspects of human resources practices, such as promotion rates by gender. One statistic is not enough to draw conclusions about turnover, promotion rates, and other key aspects of human resources practices but may call attention to areas worthy of further investigation.

AVERAGE AGE

This statistic shows the average age for employees in each employee group, men and women separately, and across EEO categories if you have chosen to add them. Like Average Years of Service, this statistic speaks to the maturity of the workforce and past human resources practices based on individual characteristics rather than the jobs held by the individuals. Distinct differences across genders or ethnic groups can indicate a need for further investigation. For example, are women almost always older than men in the same group? The new or revised compensation structure needs to include compensation policies that forestall discrimination or disparate impact as well as monitoring mechanisms.

AVERAGE SALARY

This statistic shows the average salary held by employees in that employee group, men and women separately and across EEO categories if you have chosen to add them. This statistic is important for a compensation manager and could point to one or more key areas to be targeted in the new or revised compensation structure. If one category of workers consistently has a significantly lower average salary than another group of workers in the same employee group, the compensation manager should find out why.

SPREADSHEET 4   A B C C O M M U N I T Y S E R V I C E S —
                 T H E W O R K F O R C E

Mission Statement: Provide Service to Those in Need

	A	B	C	D	E
		Employee Group	Number Full-Time	Number Part-Time	Number Variable-Time
1					
2	Exempt	Senior management: M			
3		F			
4		Middle managment: M			
5		F			
6		Professional: M			
7		F			
8		Other exempt: M			
9		F			
10		Confidential: M			
11		F			
12	Nonexempt	Administrative: M			
13		F			
14		Skilled crafts: M			
15		F			
16		Laborers: M			
17		F			
18		Other: M			
19		F			

ORG / GOV / REV / **WRKFRC** / COMP / EXMPT / NONEX / JOBS / NewCOMP / PerfMgt / MAINT

Legend:

Employee Group: Broad groupings of employees based on jobs of similar type and scope. M and F are male and female. Include any other useful demographic categories.

Number Full-Time: Number of full-time employees.

Number Part-Time: Number of part-time employees.

Number Variable-Time: Number of variable-time employees.

Appointment Terms: Employment contract, at will, represented, and other terms applicable to employees in this group.

F	G	H	I	J
Appointment Terms	Unionized	Average Years of Service	Average Age	Average Salary
	N/A			
	N/A			
	N/A			
	N/A			
	N/A			
	Y/N			
	Y/N			
	Y/N			
	Y/N			

Unionized: Group is represented by a collective bargaining unit.

Average Years of Service: Average number of years with the organization for members of this group.

Average Age: The average age of employees in this group.

Average Salary: Average base salary for employees in this group.

CHAPTER 5

Current Compensation—How Are We Paying Them Now?

In the previous chapter, the information to be collected for Spreadsheet 4, Workforce, served to test the extent and user friendliness of the organization's compensation data infrastructure. In the course of collecting this very basic information, a new compensation manager gets exposure to the human resources information system in place and may be dismayed to find that there is no system in place, or that the system is slow to respond to information requests, or is so haphazardly maintained that the information is suspect once received.

Of course, the compensation manager may be grateful to find that the human resources information system in place is fully adequate, or even better than adequate. Most of us adjust easily to good news!

HUMAN RESOURCES INFORMATION SYSTEMS INFRASTRUCTURE

A human resources information system (HRIS) typically contains both:

- Payroll information (data required to pay people correctly and meet external legal standards for reporting)
- Human resources information (data required to track and monitor the workforce from initial hire to separation)

In many cases, payroll and human resources require the same information. However, there is a difference between the two functions with respect to external requirements and internal emphasis. Payroll is a heavily regulated activity, while human resources activities such as recruitment, leave accounting, and training typically operate under less routine external scrutiny. Compensation managers are vitally interested in both kinds of information and see them as parts of a whole.

Developing an HRIS requires an analysis beyond the scope of this book. If such an endeavor confronts you, a considerable amount of time, effort, and possibly financial resources will be required to perform a comprehensive needs analysis, a product comparison against that needs analysis, vendor selection (possibly including an internal information systems unit), and implementation including staff training. A compensation manager with luck and influence with management might be able to retain an HRIS implementation specialist, a very advantageous approach.

If the compensation manager must develop a new or revised compensation structure while implementing the necessary HRIS required to describe and monitor such a structure, then the task will be doubly complicated and may require a new and expanded job description to allow for the increased scope of work.

Appendix C lists HRIS data elements suggested by successive classes in "Information and Cost Analysis in HR Management." Over a five-year period, students (mostly practicing HR professionals) built the list by adding to or revising data elements suggested by the previous classes. If you are burdened with addressing HRIS issues from scratch, then this list may provide a basis for departure.

EMPLOYEE GROUPS

The previous chapter on the workforce listed certain default employee groups, and you may have further refined these groups across gender and EEO categories to meet your own organizational needs. This fifth spreadsheet (COMP) is intended to record aspects of the organization's current compensation structure, even if management would not use the formal term *structure* to define the current pay system (see Spreadsheet 5 at the end of this chapter as well as in Appendix B).

In collecting and recording this set of information, you may need to further subdivide the employee groups from the previous chapter. If you need to maintain statistics by gender or EEO category within each group or subgroup, then you should continue to do so when structuring the COMP spreadsheet. For example, if inspection shows that women work without job descriptions far more frequently than men, or the other way around, then further investigation into disparate treatment may be indicated.

NUMBER

This column records the number of employees in the employee group or subgroup.

UNIONIZED

This column should contain the same information as shown on Spreadsheet 4, WRKFRC, unless you determine that further subgroups are necessary.

AVERAGE YEARS IN JOB

Unlike "Average Years of Service" on Spreadsheet 4, this statistic measures the average number of years that employees in that employee group or subgroup have served in their *current* jobs. This information casts light on the level of experience, promotion patterns, and emphasis on job stability in the various employee subgroups. Results in one or more groups or subgroups could indicate anomalies with respect to promotion or hiring practices. For example, this statistic could show that some employees in one group, such as white males or Hispanics, have served in their current jobs twice as long as other groups, a possible indication of adverse impact if not outright discrimination.

PAY STRUCTURE

This information should be a list of every type of pay structure applicable to employees in the group. Possibilities include a step structure, ranges without steps, flat rate, a series of flat rates based on formal qualifications such as degrees or certifications, a seniority system, and other possibilities. The compensation manager should know why certain pay structures are considered appropriate for certain employee groups, as well as how the employees in the group view these pay structures, or if the employees even know or believe that pay structures exist.

JOB DESCRIPTIONS

This column contains only three entries: All, Some, or None. If all employees in the employee group have a job description, then the column should show "All." If only some of the employees have a job description, then the column would show "Some." A "None" entry means that there are no job descriptions for any of the employees in the employee group.

SALARIES PUBLIC

Are salaries for employees in this group considered public information? Do employees either know or know how to obtain salary information on each other and on management? Do the voting public and the media have access to organizational salaries? If so, the development, approval, and implementation of the new or revised compensation system may require a public relations strategy. If a legislative body is involved, the compensation manager may spend a considerable amount of time in liaison with the external agency as well as with internal management and other employees.

PERFORMANCE MANAGEMENT

This column is similar to the "Job Description" column in that the answers are either All, Some, or None. Is there a performance management system in place for employees in this group? Employees who expect periodic performance evaluations from their managers, and managers who are practiced and methodical in doing evaluations, should be accustomed to structure in the determination of pay and related personnel actions such as promotions and reclassifications. Acceptance of one structure can pave the way to acceptance of another, particularly if the workforce perceives that the positive aspects of the current structure will be retained in its replacement.

SALARY INCREASE DATE

Do employees in this employee group become eligible for their salary increases on a common date, an individual anniversary date, a contractually determined date, whenever an employee asks for a raise, on an ad hoc basis determined by management, or on some other date?

Salary increases may be tied to the budget cycle, some point in the fiscal year, staggered at intervals throughout the year, or on some other schedule. The rhythm of this process, or lack of it, will impact the implementation of the new or revised compensation structure.

COMPENSATION AUTHORITY

This column records the organizational authority for compensation approvals for the employees in the employee group. For example, the governing board may approve the compensation arrangement for the top executive who then approves the compensation arrangements for other senior management officials. If there are differences in approval authority within a single employee group, the compensation manager should find out why. Differences in approval authority within a single employee group may suggest further subdivision of that employee group.

SPREADSHEET 5   ABC COMMUNITY SERVICES—
CURRENT COMPENSATION

Mission Statement: Provide Service to Those in Need

		Number	Unionized	Average Years in Job	Pay Structure
	Employee Group				
Exempt	Senior management		N/A		
	Middle management		N/A		
	Professional		N/A		
	Other exempt		N/A		
	Confidential		N/A		
Nonexempt	Administrative		Y/N		
	Skilled crafts		Y/N		
	Laborers		Y/N		
	Other		Y/N		

Tabs: ORG / GOV / REV / WRKFRC / **COMP** / EXMPT / NONEX / JOBS / NewCOMP / PerfMgt / MAINT

Are any or all of the following in place: an organization chart, payroll/HRIS, central HR files on all employees?

Legend:

Employee Group: Broad groupings of employees based on jobs of similar type and scope. This column should begin with the same employee groups found on the WRKFRC spreadsheet and include M, F, and EEO categories if the WRKFRC spreadsheet indicates potential EEO issues.

Number: Number of employees in this group or subgroup.

Unionized: Members of this group or subgroup represented by a collective bargaining unit.

Average Years in Job: The average number of years served in the job currently held by members of this group or subgroup.

Pay Structure: Individual negotiation, ranges, flat rate, other.

Job Descriptions: Yes (available for all employees in group), no (for no employees in group), some (only for some of the employees in the group).

G	H	I	J	K
Job Descriptions	Salaries Public	Performance Management	Salary Increase Date	Compensation Authority

Salaries Public: Are salaries for jobs in this group available to the general public? To the employee population?

Performance Management: Is there a performance management process in place for all/some/none of the employees in this group?

Salary Increase Date: When do employees in this group become eligible for base salary increases? (Common date? Anniversary? Other?)

Compensation Authority: Describe the authority level(s) for approving compensation arrangements for members of the group.

CHAPTER 6

Exempt Workforce — Your Colleagues and Your Boss

A profile of this sector of the workforce might read as follows:

- Competent and experienced
- More knowledgeable about the organizational environment than you are
- Directly affected by your project
- Possibly in a position of authority over you

Each of these profile attributes is daunting, to say the least. The compensation manager charged with creating or substantially revising the organization's compensation system may have to grapple with the political consequences of his or her role as a change agent ready to disadvantage colleagues or even upper management with respect to their compensation, or *perceived to be ready to do so*. The latter may carry the same baggage as the former.

In the real world of compensation managers, senior management is highly unlikely to permit a newly created or substantially revised compensation system to disadvantage them with respect to their pay unless compelled by overwhelming forces such as the will of the electorate, a mandate from the board, or legal sanctions. However, such overwhelming forces might exist and, in fact, be the impetus for charging the compensation manager with the project in the first place. It is possible that the compensation manager will struggle under a burden of political pressure that will make mere compensation analysis a relief. Such political pressures are outside the scope of this book, and this paragraph is intended only to acknowledge their possible existence and importance.

EMPLOYEE GROUP

In previous chapters, the Employee Group information reflected not only the basic categories of employees (exempt/nonexempt, senior/middle management, professional, etc.) but possibly various EEO categories as well. By including EEO categories on previous spreadsheets, the compensation manager has had the opportunity to test the waters with respect to possible areas of discrimination and also to test the HRIS capabilities existing in the organization. Depending on the nature of the data collected heretofore, it may or may not be useful to continue to include EEO information on the spreadsheets from now on. The compensation manager needs to weigh any possible usefulness of EEO data with the resulting complexity of the spreadsheet. Spreadsheet 6 (EXMPT) at the end of this chapter (as well as in Appendix B) assumes that the need for EEO data is no longer present, but this assumption should be ignored if your circumstances indicate otherwise.

Also, the compensation manager should decide whether to include confidential employees in the exempt workforce or in the nonexempt workforce. Strictly speaking, the "Confidential" designation applies to employees holding nonexempt jobs but excluded from otherwise applicable collective bargaining agreements due to the nature of their work. Some organizations treat employees holding such jobs at least as well or better than their unionized counterparts. Let your current organizational practice be your guide, although you may decide ultimately to recommend a change to that practice.

JOBS

This list contains every job belonging to each employee group regardless of how many incumbents, if any, hold the job. A new or vacant job under recruitment would be included in this list if a compensation arrangement exists for that job. If your organization is relatively large, this spreadsheet might go on for several pages, so you will want to format the spreadsheet to aid readability, for example, page numbers, repeating row headings, headers, and footers.

The compensation manager should note any job that is either tied to another job or another employee group with respect to compensation or is currently used, informally or formally, as a benchmark for one or more other jobs.

REVENUE IMPACT

This field evaluates the direct relationship between performance in each job and revenue. In other words, if the incumbent (or all incumbents) in the job performed superbly, what would be the *direct* effect on revenue? If the incumbent (or all incumbents) in the job performed below the minimum standard, what would be the *direct* effect on revenue? The compensation manager may have to resist peer pressure to say that all jobs matter and that revenue is dependent on everyone pulling together. Although such a statement may have merit with respect to organizational development theory, it is less than useful for compensation analysis.

Going back to the charity for the homeless, for example, the operational focus is on satisfying the needs of the homeless while the revenue focus looks in another direction altogether: The opinions and willingness to pay of individuals and groups that do not need these charitable services and may never have been to a homeless shelter. The compensation manager may have to take a hard-headed look at the operations management and staff jobs at such a charity and ask such questions as

- What percentage of the charity's donors interacted with operations management and staff *before* making their first contribution?
- What percentage of the charity's donors were volunteers *before* making their first contribution?

If the answers to these and other questions indicate that donations, that is, revenue, reach the charity more often than not without direct involvement with the operations management and staff, then these operations jobs are not directly related to revenue. This does not mean that the operations management and staff can perform in a substandard fashion over time without endangering revenue. However, it would mean that there is only an *indirect* relationship between the performance in these jobs and revenue, thereby placing revenue enhancement out of the reach of those who hold such jobs, no matter how well they perform. However, if the charity has a development office charged with donor contact and solicitation, superb performance in development jobs *would* have a direct effect on revenue enhancement, and substandard performance would have the reverse effect.

When the compensation manager begins development of the new or revised compensation structure, a realistic perspective on revenue impact for each of the various jobs will guide the designation of appropriate rewards.

BASE PAY

This field records the mechanism that determines base pay for each job. Base pay may be set according to internal pay ranges, tied to external pay ranges such as state civil service, determined by collective bargaining contracts, negotiated individually with every incumbent, set according to a flat rate determined by the board, or by some other means. The various base pay setting mechanisms may have the force of law, reflect historical accident or a legal precedent, or be completely ad hoc.

The compensation manager is charged with creating or substantially revising a compensation structure, so the existing arrangements are extremely important because to those employees, the existing arrangements are "the deal." Any proposed changes will be scrutinized by these exempt employees who will probably detect any possible disadvantages for themselves in short order.

BASE PAY INCREASES

Presumably, incumbents in these exempt jobs have received base pay increases in the past. The compensation manager will want to find out the basis on which such increases were given: seniority, longevity, cost-of-living adjustment (COLA), general increase based on the organization's ability to pay, merit, other?

If experience is a guide, most organizations claim that base pay increases are determined by merit. An astute compensation manager does not accept this assertion on face value but wants to know how merit is determined and by whom. Objective standards for merit in each job may be in place for some jobs and not for others. Such objective standards may be very difficult to establish for some jobs, making merit for performance in that job strictly in the eye of the beholder, usually a manager.

VARIABLE PAY

Do incumbents in the job receive pay increases or a portion of base pay on the basis of meeting specific goals set for the individual, a team that includes the individual, or on the achievement of organization-wide goals? If so,

- What portion of the pay increase or base pay is dependent on each possible variable pay component?
- Who determines the goals and the span of performance (individual, team, or organization-wide)?
- How long has such a system been in place?
- How is it received by incumbents?
- How is it received by the organization?

PERSON-BASED PAY

Are any incumbents in the job eligible to receive or currently receiving person-based pay for acquisitions of skills, knowledge, and/or competencies? If so,

- Who determined these skills, knowledge, and/or competencies?
- What are the skills, knowledge, and/or competencies appropriate for each job?
- Who determines that an incumbent has acquired the skill, knowledge, or competency?
- How does the evaluator make such a skills/knowledge/competency determination?
- How long has such a system been in place?
- How is it received by the incumbents?
- How is it received by the organization?

HEALTH BENEFITS

Benefits are a very complex area, and this book does not address most of the related complexities or the current turbulence in our society regarding the escalating costs of healthcare and the current and desired level of government involvement.

This field is intended to provide a list of health benefits voluntarily implemented by the organization and enjoyed by incumbents in the job. Benefits can include direct healthcare (medical, dental, vision, etc.), life insurance plans, wellness programs, employee assistance programs, and any other programs intended to improve employee well-being. If the compensation manager has doubts about whether a program should be included, such as organizational willingness to sponsor membership in a weight reduction program, it is prudent to include the benefit. The program can always be removed from the list later, if necessary.

PENSION/RETIREMENT

For the purposes of this book, retirement is a broad term applicable to all forms of old age income continuation including pensions (both defined contribution and defined benefit) and supplementary retirement plans such as 401(k) and 403(b) plans. Like health benefits, pension/retirement plans are extraordinarily complex and governed by myriad regulations. This book does not address the societal turbulence currently associated with the decisions by organizations to discontinue pension plans, disassociate such plans with paid retiree healthcare, and other issues of great current concern.

This field is intended to simply list the types of pension and other retirement-related plans for which incumbents in the job are eligible.

PERQUISITES

Perquisites are those goods and services that go with organizational employment either to all employees, to incumbents in certain jobs, or as a reward for meritorious service. Perquisites can include tickets to entertainment events, country club memberships where potential donors are likely to be found, free or cheap gas at an organization-affiliated gas station, free meals at organization events at which the incumbents serve, and other desirable goods and services. Some perquisites, such as organization-paid or subsidized health club memberships, may be perceived as either perquisites or as health-related benefits.

Also, some perquisites may be viewed by the recipients as job-related resources, such as free country-club memberships for development office staff because potential donors are members of those country clubs. Such memberships may be viewed by recipients as additional office space rather than a facility for personal enjoyment.

If such perquisites do not exist, the compensation manager will want to find out why. Reasons for the lack of perquisites could include corporate culture, board oppositions, fear of electorate reaction, or simply that senior management has never thought about the matter. The need to incorporate perquisites into the budget for each coming year may be sufficient to discourage the practice.

COMPENSATION AUTHORITY

The employees holding exempt jobs, like the other members of the workforce, are currently receiving compensation in the form of pay and benefits. Someone or some group has decided what the current compensation components should be, how pay raises are determined, how often pay raises are awarded, the time of year they are awarded, and the many other factors that determine the compensation reality known to the employees as the deal.

The compensation manager seeking to make changes to the current reality needs to exercise special diligence in obtaining information about the current and past compensation authority including archival documents such as memos, records of board decisions, and meeting summaries. Oral history could be critical, especially oral history from senior managers and board members no longer affiliated with the organization. While the compensation manager may have difficulty obtaining such oral history, extra effort may yield insights that could not have been obtained otherwise.

Compensation authority, past and present, has implications both for the immediate changes the compensation manager may seek to implement as well as future maintenance of the new system.

SPREADSHEET 6   ABC COMMUNITY SERVICES—
                 THE EXEMPT WORKFORCE

Mission Statement: Provide Service to Those in Need

	A	B	C	D	E
	Employee Group	Jobs	Revenue Impact	Base Pay	Base Pay Increases
1					
2	Senior management	Job 1			
3		Job 2			
4	Middle management	Job 1			
5		Job 2			
6	Professional	Job 1			
7		Job 2			
8	Other exempt	Job 1			
9		Job 2			
10	Confidential	Job 1			
11		Job 2			

Nonprofit Spreadsheet.xls

ORG / GOV / REV / WRKFRC / COMP \ **EXMPT** / NONEX / JOBS / NewCOMP / PerfMgt / MAINT

Legend:

Employee Group: Broad groupings of employees based on jobs of similar type and scope. Because this spreadsheet may become extensive, the compensation manager may wish to omit EEO categories unless previous spreadsheets have indicated that serious issues need to be explored. For simplicity, this spreadsheet does not display EEO categories.

Jobs: A set of duties to be performed by one or more incumbents. The job may be vacant but under recruitment.

Revenue Impact: How does performance in the job affect revenue?

Base Pay: Set according to pay ranges, individual negotiation, union contract, flat rate, other?

Base Pay Increase: Based on merit, seniority, longevity, COLA, general increase, other.

F	G	H	I	J	K
Variable Pay	Person-Based Pay	Health Benefits	Pension / Retirement	Perquisites	Compensation Authority

Variable Pay: Based on individual, team-based, organization-wide performance.

Person-Based Pay: Based on competency, knowledge, skill, other.

Health Benefits: List.

Pension/Retirement: List types such as 403(b), 457, defined benefit, defined contribution.

Perquisites: Could the organization elect to give one or more employees in this job a perquisite? Does the organization currently do so? If so, what types of perquisites? Are any perquisites explicitly forbidden?

Compensation Authority: Describe the authority level(s) for approving compensation arrangements for jobs in this group.

CHAPTER 7

Nonexempt Workforce—
The Workers

Depending on the nature of your organization, the nonexempt workforce may be much larger than the exempt workforce, about the same size, or smaller. An educational institution, for example, might have a modest nonexempt staff of clerical and custodial employees supporting a much larger exempt teaching and administrative staff, while the United States Postal Service may have a small army of nonexempt staff, much larger than the managerial/exempt portion of the workforce (see Spreadsheet 7, NONEX, at the end of this chapter as well as in Appendix B).

A prudent compensation manager will want to compare the headcount, or full-time equivalent (FTE) populations, of exempts to nonexempts and then compare the payroll costs for these same groups. The results might indicate that there are more nonexempt employees in terms of headcount and FTE, but the nonexempt portion of the payroll is actually smaller. This apparent mismatch between numbers and dollars could mean that senior management might devote the greatest share of its attention to restraining nonexempt pay, reasoning that cost control is best served by controlling pay levels for the larger group. However, cost control might be best served by controlling pay levels for the less numerous exempt employees. Should such a mistaken assumption exist in your organization, you will want to gracefully bring the statistical truth home to those who will evaluate your final proposal.

EMPLOYEE GROUP

The organization may have grouped nonexempt jobs by similar function, by collective bargaining affiliation, by organizational unit, or by some other employment attribute. Perhaps the organization has ignored these jobs and done what was necessary to recruit and retain to an acceptable level but not analyzed this portion of the workforce. If there are no *a priori* employee groups established, the compensation manager will have to establish them in order to complete the spreadsheet (NONEX) found at the end of this chapter.

Your organization may contain workers in nonexempt jobs who are represented through the collective bargaining process. Such contracts address the terms and conditions of employment for all incumbents in certain jobs, an automatic employee group. If your organization has more than one union contract, then the employees covered by each separate contract will be in separate employee groups.

JOBS

Within each employee group are one or more jobs, and these should be listed in a manner similar to the listing of exempt jobs on the spreadsheet at the end of Chapter 6. That is, each job is listed whether there is an incumbent or not. New and vacant jobs under recruitment should be listed because compensation arrangements exist for those jobs.

The compensation manager should note any job that is either tied to another job or employee group with respect to compensation or is currently used, informally or formally, as a benchmark for one or more other jobs. For example, a collective bargaining contract may determine the compensation for all jobs within a particular employee group, but selected jobs within another employee group may be tied, by organizational policy or practice, to the compensation structure determined by the collective bargaining contract.

REVENUE IMPACT

The test for revenue impact is the same for nonexempt jobs as for exempt jobs: a direct relationship between performance in the job and organizational revenue. The compensation manager cannot assume that performance in any one nonexempt job has no direct effect on revenue, whatever its place in the organizational hierarchy. However humbling the insight may be, a postal worker who deals with the public by affixing proper postage to letters and packages as well as selling stamps may be actually closer to the organization's revenue stream than a compensation manager. Each job must be analyzed without preconception as to its impact on the organization's revenue stream.

BASE PAY

This information shows how base pay for the job is determined. Options include existing pay ranges, individual negotiation, union negotiation, existing flat rates, pay at other organizations, external labor market rates according to one or more surveys, other factors, or some combination. The compensation manager will want to be particularly sensitive to different methods being used to determine base pay within an employee group or, even more troublesome, among incumbents within a single job.

BASE PAY INCREASE

No doubt the existing employees have been receiving increases to their base pay from time to time, and the compensation manager needs to know how these increases were determined. Options include merit, seniority, longevity, cost-of-living, general increase, external job surveys, other, or some combination. Once again, the compensation manager should be sensitive to differences in the manner in which base pay increases are determined among jobs within employee groups or among incumbents in a single job.

The compensation manager will also want to be sensitive to labels that do not match practical reality, such as "merit increases" that are the same or substantially the same for all incumbents in all or some of the jobs within an employee group, or across all incumbents within a specific job.

VARIABLE PAY

Are any of the nonexempt employee groups, or incumbents within a single nonexempt job, eligible for variable pay in whole or in part on the basis of

- Achievement of individual goals
- Achievement of goals for a team to which they belong
- Overall organizational achievement

If a system of variable pay for one or more nonexempt jobs is currently in place, the compensation manager will want to see how "variable" the rewards actually are.

Are the goals and achievements on which these variable awards are based truly within the line of sight of these employees? If the goals are team-based, how are the reward amounts determined? Where does the money come from? If the goals are organization-wide, how are the reward amounts distributed throughout the organization? Who determines the amounts or the timing of the rewards? Variable rewards may lend themselves to variable impact on employee compensation, and the compensation manager needs all the details on any such existing reward components.

PERSON-BASED PAY

Are any nonexempt employees currently eligible for person-based pay either on the acquisition of additional skills, knowledge, or competencies? If so, what jobs are involved? Who decides which skills, knowledge, or competencies for each job or employee group are appropriate? How do the current collective bargaining contracts acknowledge such person-based pay components, if at all?

HEALTH BENEFITS

Benefits are a very complex area, and this book does not address most of the complexities or the current turbulence in our society regarding escalating costs of health benefits and the current and desired level of government involvement.

This field is intended to provide a list of benefits enjoyed by incumbents in the job and would include direct healthcare insurance programs (medical, dental, vision, etc.), life insurance plans, as well as wellness programs, employee assistance programs, and any other programs intended to improve employee well-being. If the compensation manager has doubts about whether a program should be included, such as organizational willingness to sponsor membership in a weight reduction program, it is prudent to include the benefit. The program can always be removed from the list later, if necessary.

The compensation manager should be especially sensitive to any differences in healthcare benefits between the exempt jobs and the nonexempt jobs.

PENSION/RETIREMENT

For the purposes of this book, retirement is a broad term applicable to all organizations and including pensions (both defined contribution and defined benefit) and supplementary retirement plans such as 401(k) and 403(b) plans. Like health benefits, pension/retirement plans are extraordinarily complex and governed by myriad regulations. This book does not address the societal turbulence currently associated with the decisions by organizations to discontinue pension plans, disassociate such plans with paid retiree healthcare, and other issues of great current concern. This field is intended to simply list the types of pension and other retirement-related plans for which incumbents in the job are eligible.

The compensation manager should be especially sensitive to differences in retirement policy or practice between exempt and nonexempt jobs.

PERQUISITES

Perquisites are those goods and services that go with organizational employment either to all employees, to incumbents in certain jobs, or as a reward for meritorious service. Perquisites can include tickets to entertainment events, country club memberships where potential donors are likely to be found, free or cheap gas at an organization-affiliated gas station, free meals at organization events at which the incumbents serve, and other desirable goods and services. Some perquisites, such as organization-paid or subsidized health club memberships, may be perceived as either perquisites or as health benefits.

The compensation manager will want to be especially sensitive to perquisites available to employees on the basis of perceived income levels, such as free meals to those holding certain jobs but not to others. Also, some perquisites may be viewed by the recipients as job-related resources, such as free country club memberships for development office staff because potential donors are members of those country clubs. Such memberships may be viewed by recipients as additional office space rather than a facility for personal enjoyment.

If such perquisites do not exist, the compensation manager should find out why. Reasons for the lack of perquisites could include corporate culture, board opposition, fear of electorate reaction, or simply that senior management has never thought about the matter. The need to incorporate perquisites into the budget for each coming year may be sufficient to discourage the practice.

COMPENSATION AUTHORITY

The employees holding nonexempt jobs, like the other members of the workforce, are currently receiving compensation in the form of pay and benefits. Someone or some group (including a collective bargaining contract) has decided what the current compensation components should be, how pay raises are determined, how often pay raises are awarded, the time of year they are awarded, and the myriad of other factors that determine the current compensation reality.

The compensation manager seeking to make changes to the current reality will need to exercise special diligence in obtaining information about the current and past compensation authority including archival documents such as memos, records of board decisions, and meeting summaries. Has responsibility for determining compensation arrangements for nonexempt workers been historically placed in one person, possibly a lower level manager? How much authority and flexibility do lower level supervisors have in determining compensation arrangements for their employees, or even to giving pay increases?

Oral history could be critical, especially oral history from managers and board members no longer affiliated with the organization. While the compensation manager may have difficulty obtaining such oral history, extra effort may yield insights that could not have been obtained otherwise.

Compensation authority, past and present, has implications for the immediate changes the compensation manager may seek to implement as well as the maintenance of the system in the future and employee morale throughout the process.

SPREADSHEET 7   **ABC COMMUNITY SERVICES—
THE NONEXEMPT WORKFORCE**

Mission Statement: Provide Service to Those in Need

	A	B	C	D	E
					Base Pay
1	Employee Group	Jobs	Revenue Impact	Base Pay	Increase
2	Administrative	Job A			
3		Job B			
4	Skilled crafts	Job A			
5		Job B			
6	Laborers	Job A			
7		Job B			
8	Other unionized	Job A			
9		Job B			

Nonprofit Spreadsheet.xls

Tabs: ORG / GOV / REV / WRKFRC / COMP / EXMPT \ **NONEX** / JOBS / NewCOMP / PerfMgt / MAINT

Legend:

Employee Group: Broad groupings of employees based on Jobs of similar type and scope. Because this spreadsheet may become extensive, the compensation manager may wish to omit EEO categories unless previous spreadsheets have indicated that serious issues need to be explored.

Job: A set of duties, or job, held by one or more employees or vacant but under recruitment.

Revenue Impact: How does performance in the Job affect revenue?

Base Pay: Set according to pay ranges, individual negotiation, union contract, flat rate, other?

Base Pay Increase: Based on merit, seniority, longevity, COLA, general increase, other?

Variable Pay: Based on performance as an individual, team member, organization member.

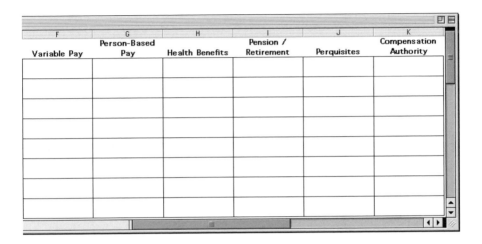

Person-Based: Competency, knowledge, skill.

Health Benefits: List.

Pension/Retirement: List type(s), such as 403(b), 457, defined benefit, defined contributions, and so on.

Perquisites: Could the organization elect to give one or more employees in this Job a perquisite? Does the organization currently do so? If so, what types of perquisites? Are any perquisites explicitly forbidden?

Compensation Authority: Describe the authority level(s) for approving compensation arrangements for Jobs in this group.

CHAPTER 8

Jobs—Job Analysis: Finally!

The compensation manager might well turn to job analysis with a sigh of relief, anticipating the relaxing company of an old acquaintance after making so many testy new ones, such as the budget process and the approval role of a governing board. This relief may be short-lived.

One could make the case that job analysis is the linchpin of human resources management, a pivotal effort impacting several human resources activities including employment, workforce planning, Americans with Disabilities Act accommodations, and our old friend, compensation analysis. It is possible that a comprehensive job analysis has already been completed in recent organizational memory and that previous effort may have been traumatic. Senior management may not want to revisit a major effort even if it was well-received, but the prudent compensation manager does not take without question the previous conclusions of another professional, however able. Therefore, a job analysis is probably in your immediate future, at least with respect to the job description and job specifications.

Advance planning for the job analysis effort means that the compensation manager has networked with colleagues and management enough to know who can (and will) serve as a court of last resort when a contested job description and specifications require a final approval. Employees naturally want their own job descriptions to qualify for as high a salary level as possible by whatever job analysis method is used. Supervisors and managers may want to aggrandize their own roles by "puffing" the job descriptions and related specifications for their employees' job descriptions as well as for their own. The compensation manager needs an understanding and resolute senior manager, committee, or outside opinion—or some combination thereof—to resolve and confirm the job analysis results.

EMPLOYEE GROUP

The employee groups listed on Spreadsheet 8 (JOBS) (shown at the end of this chapter and in Appendix B) should be those identified on earlier spreadsheets. If previous EEO subgroups have indicated any serious problems with respect to discrimination or adverse impact, then the compensation manager may want to continue displaying the EEO categories on this spreadsheet. Due to the potential complexity of Spreadsheet 8, the compensation manager may need to keep any EEO or related demographic analysis separate from the job analysis effort. The JOBS spreadsheet will be complex enough, and a simpler format with fewer groups and subgroups may be more self-evident to senior managers who have neither the time nor the inclination to sort out a complicated matrix.

Of course, the compensation manager can retain EEO subcategories on the JOBS spreadsheet and use the Hide Columns or Hide Rows features for display purposes.

JOBS

Every job in the organization, exempt and nonexempt, would be listed on this spreadsheet by employee group.

NUMBER OF INCUMBENTS

This column displays the number of incumbents in each job. Senior management or the compensation manager may want to examine the jobs with the largest number of incumbents first, or last, or in some other strategic order. The decision to analyze jobs in a particular order is only one of the many job analysis decisions to be made by the compensation manager. There may be related organizational implications, such as the determination of when to analyze senior management jobs.

REVENUE IMPACT

The revenue impact of each job—the relationship between performance in the job and organizational revenue—has already been determined and displayed on the EXEMPT and NONEX spreadsheets. Because the JOBS spreadsheet is intended to provide all relevant job analysis information on one spreadsheet, revenue impact is included on the JOBS spreadsheet, as well.

JOB ANALYSIS: JOB DESCRIPTIONS

Job descriptions either exist, or they don't. If they exist, they are either current, or they aren't.

Is anything ever this simple?

The organization may believe that everyone has a job description. Close inspection of these job descriptions may reveal omission of certain key information, outdated information in one or more fields, and other anomalies. Some organizations are aware only of certain components of the job description. As long as the incumbent's name and the job title have not changed, the job description looks current.

According to the Society for Human Resource Management certification preparation materials,[1] typical job descriptions include the following elements:

- FLSA status (exempt or nonexempt)
- Department
- Reporting relationship
- Job summary: four or five sentences summarizing the overall purpose and objectives of the job and addressing results to be achieved and degree of freedom to act
- General purpose: major functions, for example, strategic management, customer relations
- Role qualifications: the broad description of the organizational role the incumbent must play, for example, "address customer issues and ensure effective and long-term problem resolution"[2]

- Job responsibilities: the tasks, duties, and responsibilities of the job
- Essential skills and experience: those tasks, duties, and responsibilities required for the job and why
- Nonessential skills and experience: desirable, but not necessary, aspects of the job
- Supervisory responsibilities: titles of direct reports and possibly some indication of indirect reports
- Physical demands and working environment: the environment in which the work is performed, especially if unpleasant or dangerous
- Minimum qualifications: minimum knowledge, skills, and abilities required to enter the job
- Success factors: personal characteristics that contribute to an individual's ability to perform well in the job

Your organization may need more, fewer, or even different elements, and you will want to analyze your organization's job description needs carefully.

The organization may have job descriptions for some or all of the jobs. If so, the compensation manager must have some standard for currency. Jobs often change when incumbents change, and may change even when incumbents remain in the job. The stable nature of the public and non-profit environments may work to the compensation manager's advantage in this case, and a judicious analysis could show that most job descriptions are sufficiently current to be accepted.

It is possible that senior management will underestimate the time necessary to evaluate the "current" job descriptions with respect to their accuracy. Senior management may even be impatient with additional staff time spent on these descriptions, either in creation or verification. This impatience is especially likely when jobs have been held for a long time by a single individual, so that the job and the person have become identical in management perception. However, the compensation manager will want the new or revised compensation structure to rest on a rock-solid base, and that base is the result of job analysis. *Job descriptions contested and resented by incumbents or ignored by their supervisors are worse than useless.*

The previous paragraphs have made the happy assumption that a previous job analysis has occurred within some reasonable timeframe and that at least some of the resulting job descriptions are acceptably current. Unfortunately, it is possible that the compensation manager faces an organization that has never conducted an organization-wide job analysis, creating abbreviated job descriptions only when necessary for recruitment, such as a newspaper job advertisement. If there has been no prior job analysis effort, then the compensation manager must start from the beginning and, depending on the size of the organization, face a demanding effort. There may be an advantage to this circumstance if senior management accepts the need for a job analysis, knows that no such analysis has been done, and accepts the logic that the compensation manager and staff must devote a significant amount of time and effort to that end.

The creation of job descriptions seems to blend art and science, and the compensation manager must exercise technical competence as well as sensitivity to both the workforce and the organization to analyze the jobs properly. Compensation textbooks contain suggestions for the creation of job descriptions including observation, interviews with incumbents and supervisors, questionnaires, and other approaches. The size of the organization, the number of geographic locations, and the nature of the workforce are some of the factors that affect the techniques selected. For example, a job in which the incumbents are from various countries and speak little English might make questionnaires and interviews more complicated.

This column may contain the level of detail desired such as the date the job description was completed, an X to show that there is a generic job description, reporting relationships, or any other job description information.

JOB ANALYSIS: JOB SPECIFICATIONS

An outgrowth of the job description, job specifications detail the qualifications necessary to perform the job including experience and related education or training; knowledge/skills/abilities; physical and mental demands; and the level of responsibility held by the incumbent(s). The compensation manager may encounter an inclination on the part of management and staff to express the specifications for superb performance rather than satisfactory performance. This inclination could be expressed by the incumbent, who wants the job to appear as challenging as possible, the incumbent's supervisor who wants the supervisory responsibility vis-à-vis the job to appear as prestigious as possible, or upper management, which may have long identified the job with a specific and exceptionally able incumbent.

The development of job specifications gives the compensation manager the opportunity to identify success factors and, in turn, performance review criteria. Performance management will be greatly enhanced by agreement on even general performance criteria as part of the job analysis process.

This column may contain key qualifications for the job, an X to show that specifications have been identified, the date the job specifications were finalized, or any other job specification information.

JOB EVALUATION: ON HAVING A POINT OF VIEW

The compensation manager typically looks at jobs first and people second. Empty jobs are "live" to human resources professionals because such jobs typically require their attention through activities such as recruitment, budgetary analysis, reevaluation with respect to placement in the organizational hierarchy as well as appropriate salary level, extension approvals if recruitment is to be postponed, or even formal disestablishment. Unfilled jobs can mean budgetary allocations that remain unspent on salary and related benefits, and this unspent compensation may be available for other purposes unless or until the job is filled. Unfilled jobs can be very live, indeed.

Oh yes, sometimes there are people doing the jobs! But that is another set of issues. At the moment, we are looking at jobs as they are specified through a job analysis process with no regard to how well the incumbent performs in the job, or even if there is an incumbent at all.

In order to select the appropriate job evaluation method, the compensation manger should consider the size of the organization. Perhaps you have already formed an opinion as to the size of the organization: small, medium, or large. At the risk of oversimplification, this categorization can guide the compensation manager in selecting the appropriate job evaluation method for the organization or, if the organization is sufficiently large and diverse, for each employee group within the organization. Evaluating the organization with respect to size and complexity requires a balance among factors such as size of the workforce, the number of jobs, presence or absence of union contracts, and other factors unique to the organizational environment.

How big is big? As a rule of thumb, I would suggest that any public or nonprofit workforce of more than 500 workers merits special attention when selecting job evaluation methods for one or more employee groups. This rule of thumb is probably laughable to most readers from the world of government or higher education where workforces of thousands, or more, are common.

An organization with fewer than 500 employees might be sufficiently diversified and qualify as big. For example, a clinic providing healthcare to low-income and older citizens might have relatively highly paid healthcare professionals, service workers covered by union contracts, security personnel, and both exempt and nonexempt workers such as accounting and human resources professionals. There could be several employee groups in such an organization. Now assume that this nonprofit organization is operated by a specific religious group. There may be additional compensation assumptions due to membership in one or more religious orders.

Similarly, an organization with more than 500 workers might be rather simple with respect to the number of jobs. A large food service operating meals-on-wheels for low-income seniors in multiple locations might employ cooks, delivery personnel, and a very minimal administrative staff. If there are no union, religious, or other special considerations, the number of jobs requiring evaluation might be quite minimal and the job evaluation method selected accordingly.

Will the organization be big tomorrow?

If the organization is on the threshold of a size or complexity that could qualify as "big," then the possibility of future growth must be considered. In such a case, the compensation manager will want to talk to senior management, members of the governing board if applicable, and colleagues as to the likelihood that the organization will increase in size and complexity. Saddling a smaller organization with a complicated job evaluation method requiring significant maintenance beyond its resources is inappropriate. However, equally inappropriate is the selection of a simpler and more intuitive job evaluation method for a large organization with multiple unions, sophisticated and possibly contentious employees, and strong growth potential.

The following job evaluation methods fall into two categories: nonquantitative and quantitative. Nonquantitative job evaluation methods look at the whole job and evaluate its relationship to other whole jobs. Quantitative job evaluation methods evaluate all jobs according to a single set of factors and arrive at a number assigned to that job. All the jobs can then be ranked according to their respective scores.

NONQUANTITATIVE JOB EVALUATION METHODS

There are two nonquantitative job evaluation methods described in this book:

1. Ranking
2. Job Classification

Both job evaluation methods work well for organizations without sufficient resources to commit to the job evaluation process, even if the organization is quite large.

Ranking means comparing each job to every other job, resulting in a ranking from the highest level job to the lowest level job. In simpler organizations, the resulting hierarchy of jobs may even be self-evident and unlikely to spark controversy. However, ranking does not lend itself to justification for the relative value of the jobs to the organization, and that relative value will greatly affect the assignment of salary grades or rates to each job. The compensation manager, to say nothing of supervisors and managers, may be hard pressed to say why Job 5 is paid at twice the level as Job 6 which, in turn, is paid only 10 percent more than Job 7.

Job classification is a job evaluation method quite familiar to government employees who may live and work within such a system for their entire careers. Jobs are evaluated as whole jobs and placed in grades or classifications, and there may be many jobs in each classification. Within each class is at least one benchmark job that represents the entire classification due to its large number of incumbents, presence in a wide variety of employers, and general acceptance as a basis for setting wages when external rates are surveyed.

According to the SHRM Learning System, employees typically understand and accept a classification system, and the system itself can be flexible with respect to changing duties and responsibilities even if many jobs are involved. However, the system rests on the descriptions of each classification, or grade, and these classification descriptions can be overlapping. Further, unless documentation is retained to record decisions regarding the placement of jobs in the classifications and the descriptions of the classifications themselves, the job classification evaluation method can be difficult to justify.

QUANTITATIVE JOB EVALUATION METHODS

The two quantitative job evaluation methods presented here are:

1. Point-factor
2. Factor comparison

Both methods use numeric ratings to compare jobs with respect to both hierarchy and relative value.

Point-factor job evaluation begins with the selection of a set of factors by which all jobs are evaluated. The *SHRM Learning System* (2004) recommends that the organization use the compensable factors included in the Equal Pay Act and Title VII of the Civil Rights Act: skill, responsibility, effort, working conditions, and supervision of others. Your organization may wish to add other factors as well.

The selection of the compensable factors should be time consuming. Failure to include a compensable factor would severely compromise any new or revised compensation structure based on the job evaluation method. Some factors may be unique to the organization, such as creativity in an

entertainment studio or physical fitness for a trainer in a health club. Whatever compensable factors are selected, time spent in discussion with managers, supervisors, unions if present, and other groups such as employee
focus groups will be time well spent. If one or more governing board
members are involved in the effort, the compensation manager may want
to honor their role by consulting with them first and then again before fi-
nalizing the factors. If there is a legislative approval process or a committee
appointed to represent voter interests, then the compensation structure effort may be monitored from beginning to end. No technical expertise can
bypass the opinions and approvals of the governing board members or legislative representatives.

Once the compensable factors are selected, degrees of skill mastery are
assigned to each factor. These degrees of skill mastery can range from 1 (the
lowest) to 5 (the highest), with points associated with each level. The
SHRM Learning System 2004 provides the following example:

Factors	Degrees/Points				
	1	2	3	4	5
Skill	60	120	180	240	300
Responsibility	60	120	180	240	300
Effort	50	100	150	200	300
Working conditions	30	60	100	100	100
Supervision	20	40	60	80	100

Source: SHRM Learning System 2004, Module Four, Compensation and Benefits, p. 47. Reprinted
with permission.

What does this chart tell us about the organization? This organization
values skill, responsibility, and effort more than it values working conditions or supervision. There is nothing right or wrong about the relative
weighting of the points per factor per degree of mastery. However, the
compensation manager will want to think through the implications of the
relative weighting on behalf of the organization with the same careful at-

tention shown when selecting the compensable factors. An organization that does not value, that is, *pay* for, supervision may experience a reluctance on the part of workers to accept supervisory responsibilities, especially in a litigious society! Overcoming this reluctance does not mean that the organization has to add points to this factor. Instead, the organization could tie promotional opportunities to supervisory experience as potential future compensation for assuming supervisory burdens. Here again, the compensation manager should think through the implications of the point assignment to each compensable factor across the degrees of skill mastery and then acquaint all stakeholders with the implications of that point assignment. *In general, the workforce tends to concentrate effort in those areas with the most points.*

Once the organization has agreed on a framework of compensable factors, degrees of mastery, and associated points, the compensation manager and staff can analyze each job according to the accepted framework and assign points for that particular job. Point totals make the relative hierarchy and value of each job quite clear. This clarity and logic make this job evaluation method as objective as possible. However, the effort and consensus required to set up the framework is extensive and rests on clear and consistent job descriptions. Maintenance is ongoing and detailed, especially if market rates change.

As for workforce acceptance, the logical building blocks of this approach to job evaluation, so dear to the hearts of compensation managers, may quickly exhaust the patience of the workforce or, even worse, senior management, governing boards, and representatives of the electorate. Finding a simple way to express the point-factor job evaluation method may be challenging.

Factor-comparison job evaluation assigns a wage rate to each compensable factor, then builds an overall rate for the job. This method is most useful in a stable labor market. Factor-comparison is a resource-intensive job evaluation method and difficult to explain to the workforce, senior management, and even to other human resources professionals. The compensation manager may look askance at this method and wonder why such a complex and time-consuming method is useful when the labor market is stable.

The following table illustrates the development of an hourly rate for Jobs A and B:

	Skill	Responsibility	Effort	Working Conditions	Supervision
2.40	A		A		A
1.80		A		A	
1.20	B	B	B	B	
.90					B

Job A = 2.40 + 1.80 + 2.40 + 1.80 + 2.40 = $10.80/hour
Job B = 1.20 + 1.20 + 1.20 + 1.20 + .90 = $5.70/hour

Source: SHRM Learning System 2004, Module Four, Compensation and Benefits, p. 48. Reprinted with permission.

The quantitative job evaluation methods just described are quite popular in some environments and appeal to managers who are numbers-oriented and attuned to building logical systems. In my experience, most compensation managers fall into this category. However, the burden of maintenance imposed by these job evaluation methods must be carefully weighed against the perceived benefits, particularly if any senior managers, governing board members, or representatives of the electorate indicate a reluctance to either explain or maintain a compensation structure based on quantitative job evaluation methods.

OTHER

The organization may have created or adopted another job evaluation method that has worked well, such as slotting any new jobs in between jobs of greater and lesser values. If the organization already uses a defensible and robust but unusual job evaluation method that suits the current and likely future workforce, the compensation manager need not make it a point of pride to introduce a new method.

The compensation manager may want to simply check the column identifying the job evaluation method used; note relative ranking, classification assignment, or points; or enter some other job evaluation information.

NOTES

1. *The SHRM Learning System,* Module Two, Workforce Planning and Employment, pp. 90–91.
2. Ibid.

SPREADSHEET 8   ABC COMMUNITY SERVICES—
THE JOBS

Mission Statement: Provide Service to Those in Need

	Employee Group	Jobs	Number of Incumbents	Revenue Impact	Job Analysis	
					Job Description	Job Specifications
Exempt	Senior management	Job 1				
		Job 2				
	Middle management	Job 1				
		Job 2				
	Professional	Job 1				
		Job 2				
	Other exempt	Job 1				
		Job 2				
	Confidential	Job 1				
		Job 2				
Nonexempt	Administrative	Job A				
		Job B				
	Skilled crafts	Job A				
		Job B				
	Laborers	Job A				
		Job B				
	Other unionized	Job A				
		Job B				

Tabs: ORG / GOV / REV / WRKFRC / COMP / EXMPT / NONEX \ **JOBS** / NewCOMP / PerfMgt / MAINT

Legend:

Employee Group: Broad groupings of employees based on jobs of similar type and scope. This column should begin with the same employee groups found on the WRKFRC spreadsheet and include M, F, and EEO categories if the WRKFRC spreadsheet indicates potential EEO issues.

Job: A set of duties, or job, held by one or more employees or vacant but under recruitment.

Number of Incumbents: The number of employees who hold this job.

Revenue Impact: How does performance in the job affect revenue?

Job Description: A summary of a job's purpose and its tasks, duties, and responsibilities.

Job Specifications: Skills, knowledge, and abilities required for the job.

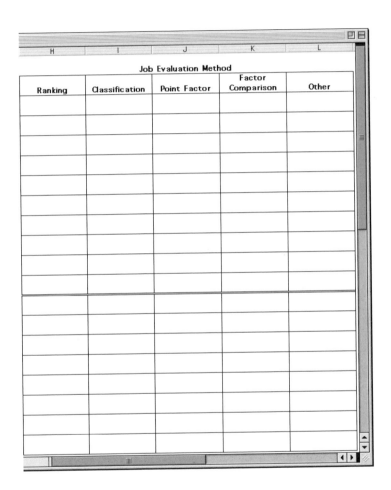

Ranking: A collection of job content evaluation techniques that compare jobs with each other or against general criteria.

Classification: A whole job evaluation technique that places jobs into grades or classifications on the basis of at least one benchmark job per grade.

Point Method: A quantitative job evaluation technique assigning points to compensable factors that describe jobs.

Factor Comparison: Selection of compensable factors for each job, then ranking all jobs by factor.

Other: For example, slotting.

CHAPTER 9

New Compensation Structure— Getting Down to Business

Acompensation manager with solid skills (or access to staff with such skills) might look at this part of the project as a long-delayed opportunity to get down to business and on with the job. The construction of ranges, evaluation of the external labor markets, and other technical compensation tasks are familiar ground. However, we aren't quite ready for those tasks yet.

THE "REAL" REASON WHY YOU'RE HERE

There is probably a simply stated reason why you have been recruited and hired to substantially revise or establish a compensation structure for the organization. If you are lucky, this simple reason reflects a practical consideration such as the expectation of abrupt future growth, preparation for a substantial change in operations, or a desire to have a different type of workforce. However, you may have been called to duty for a highly personal or political reason, a reason that cannot be spoken out loud, written down, or even communicated directly to applicants for the job you now hold.

Such hidden reasons may reflect the nature of the environment and its mission. The following hypothetical reasons are only a sample of all possible hidden reasons:

- The electorate believes that no government employee displays superior performance and will not accept substantial merit increases based on performance, no matter what documentation exists. Yet the agency is required to pay for performance.

- The electorate believes that no government employee displays superior performance, so it is politically impossible to introduce variable pay or bonuses in the organization. Yet there are pressures to modernize the agency's current compensation structure.

- The general public believes that employees in the public and non-profit environments have made a conscious trade-off between job stability and performance-based employment and therefore do not expect or deserve the same kind of salaries paid in the for-profit world for the same work, no matter what levels of performance they display. Therefore, as a practical concern, it doesn't matter what the external labor market pays because the organization should not try to meet the market unless disaster looms for compelling recruitment or retention reasons. Yet, the organization must monitor and publicly report on the relationship between its compensation levels and external labor market rates, even though the relationship has no predictable or even observable effect on its salary increase budget.

- The new chair of the governing board believes that two very large donations are likely to become reality in the next six months. The two donors want proof that the organization will keep the lid on salaries. Both donors are from the private sector and expect to see a compensation system that looks like the compensation structures normally seen in for-profit environments, at least on paper.

- Even though the organization is statutorily independent from state government, the state has control over the salary budget. If salary levels are perceived by state government workers to be more advantageous in the organization than in the state civil service, certain individuals in state government are in a position to retaliate by placing roadblocks in the organization's budget requests. Therefore, the compensation manager is expected to devise a structure that will disguise bonuses either through complicated approval processes or by labeling the bonuses as some other payment.

- The new top executive in the organization is making twice what the previous incumbent made and significantly more than top executives in comparable nonprofit organizations. To obscure this reality, the new top executive wants to overhaul the entire compensation system with the intention of providing "salary growth" possibilities for all employees with wide ranges or broadbanding. In fact, employees will be paid at the bottom of their respective ranges while the top executive is paid at the maximum of the executive range.

I hope that your *raison d'etre* falls into the category of straightforward operational imperatives rather than hidden reasons like these last six bullet points. It is crucial for your long-term career goals that you know without confusion what the new or revised compensation structure is supposed to accomplish, even if you cannot speak the reason out loud to anyone.

The preceding chapters have outlined an organizational and job analysis intended to provide the compensation manager with a list of all the jobs in the organization as well as their relative value. It should be possible to develop an organization chart from the reporting relationships identified in job descriptions. In addition, the job analysis process may point to some desirable revisions to the employee groups that have existed in the organization until now and have appeared on previous spreadsheets.

Spreadsheet 9 (NewCOMP) at the end of this chapter (as well as in Appendix B) lists the same employee groups that have appeared on previous spreadsheets. However, the compensation manager may find that it is time to revise these employee groups, or the jobs within each employee group, or both. Therefore, although employee groups on the NewCOMP spreadsheet at the end of this chapter appear unchanged from those on previous spreadsheets, your organization's employee group/job structure shown in your NewCOMP may be different, reflecting instead a revised grouping of employees and jobs. (If these revisions are sweeping and involve multiple employee groups, you will want to coordinate closely with the person in charge of human resources policies to review terms and conditions of appointment for employees in the same group.)

The following paragraphs address the basic compensation structures and related practical considerations for public or nonprofit environments, both pro and con. I know of no foolproof rules for applying various compensation structures in the public and nonprofit environments—or in for-profit environments, for that matter. The prudent compensation manager should take this one last opportunity to discuss the ramifications of each compensation arrangement with senior management, governing board members, internal and external colleagues, and any other reliable resources.

ANCILLARY PAY

Ancillary pay includes add-ons to the hourly rates for nonexempt jobs: overtime (straight time, double time, time-and-a-half, triple time, etc.), shift differentials, on-call rates, call back rates, certification or degree-earned differentials, and any other kind of special pay to be added to the hourly rate. Normally, ancillary pay is rooted in compensation policy, statutory requirements, or labor contracts.

This book assumes that these add-ons will be addressed in conformance with statutory and other requirements including organizational priorities. While the applicability of each type of ancillary pay must be documented and implemented accordingly, this book does not treat ancillary pay as part of the compensation structure.

FLAT RATES

A flat rate salary structure means that all incumbents in a specific job receive the same pay. Often such jobs are entry level or involve physical labor, skilled or unskilled. The advantages of such a structure include ease of administration and perceived fairness by the incumbents. When salary increases are contemplated, it is a straightforward matter to first determine how much various salary rate increases will cost overall and then to administer the desired salary increase. The disadvantage of the flat rate salary structure is that there is no way to reward superior performance, assuming that the nature of the job even permits observation and measuring of performance. Using a flat rate can work well at the entry level because employees are typically promoted out of the job relatively early in their tenure with the organization.

If your organization has jobs for which performance is difficult to determine beyond adherence to procedures, attendance, or other behavioral objectives, then a flat rate structure may be useful. In addition, some union contracts mandate a flat rate salary structure.

Flat Rates for Jobs in Series

Some jobs are linked in a series, each successive level of the series indicating a higher level of skill mastery. Examples of jobs in series include skilled trades with the apprentice/journeyman/master levels and the assistant/associate/full librarian titles. When there is only one salary rate for each level, then the compensation structure acts as a series of flat rates. The same advantages and disadvantages cited in the preceding section on flat rates apply to the salary rates for jobs in series. However, the potential for upward salary growth is built into the structure through the possibility of promotion within the series.

Salary Ranges

Before constructing a salary range, it is necessary to determine whether the organization will be well served by salary ranges, either with or without steps, for the particular employee group(s) in question. It falls to the compensation manager to identify the criteria by which one can determine whether the organization is well served.

How will a compensation manager know whether the organization is truly comfortable with these implications of a salary range? Among other indicators, the compensation manager will want to draw on conversations with senior managers and governing board members as well as the information displayed on previous spreadsheets. How does the revenue arrive and with what strings attached, if any? How much authority does the organization actually have to take funds coming into the organization and turn those funds into salary increases? How important is the cosmetic effect of salary ranges, even if employees move through the ranges in lockstep fashion?

A salary range implies certain aspects of compensation administration that may or may not bring comfort to your organization. For example, the top of the range says that jobs paid within this range can be worth no more than the top of the range, no matter how well they are performed. Similarly, any incumbent in any of the jobs paid within the range is entitled to at least the minimum of salary range, regardless of how inexperienced or poorly performing the incumbent may be. Jobs belonging to higher salary ranges are so placed because the work performed in those jobs is more valuable to the organization than the work performed in lower salary ranges. Is your organization comfortable in communicating these realities?

Is your organization prepared to tell incumbents paid at the top of the applicable salary range that the next salary adjustment cycle will not include them? If not, is your organization prepared to implement some mechanism, such as longevity increases, to circumvent the top of the range? Is your organization ready and able to move the ranges from time to time so that even incumbents at the top of the range will receive a salary increase? If the answer to these questions is no, then you may want to revisit the advisability of a salary range-based compensation structure.

Another implication of a salary range is that each incumbent paid within that range may view every rate within the range as attainable. Managers and supervisors may, in turn, view every rate within the range as available to be awarded to their top performers, especially if the organization espouses a pay-for-performance philosophy. If such an organization then actually pays incumbents according to some other philosophy, such as seniority or across-the-board merit increases, the workforce will learn to look askance at any and all aspects of the compensation structure because organizational philosophy and behavior are far apart.

How much authority do hiring managers have with respect to salary offers made to successful applicants? Salary rates at initial hire are often controlled by a hiring policy stipulating that no new hire may be paid more than the midpoint of the applicable salary range without special approvals. In some cases, all new hires must enter at the bottom of the applicable range. In the latter case, the salary range is virtually a flat rate for new hires, and the range spread is experienced by the new hire and the hiring manager as more hypothetical than real.

One advantage of a salary range is its appearance: Both internal and external observers expect to see salary ranges as part of a compensation structure. If the electorate, governing board, or other entities with control or influence over the organization have this view, then the compensation manager will probably include salary ranges in the revised or new compensation structure.

SALARY RANGES WITH STEPS

A compromise between the salary range and the flat rate is the salary range with steps. Assuming that the organization devises and communicates a policy dictating progression through the steps, both managers and incumbents have a more accurate picture of the intent of the salary range and what they can expect. There may be a performance aspect to progression through the steps, such as a one-step increase for satisfactory performance, a half-step salary increase to indicate that improvement is needed, and a step-and-a-half for superior performance. Government agencies, higher education institutions, and other organizations may use salary ranges with steps.

BROADBANDING

The broadband is a very large salary range frequently developed by combining several smaller ranges and includes the jobs formerly associated with these smaller salary ranges. Broadbanding was introduced as a compensation structure technique designed to support the flattening of the organization and reduce the constraints imposed by job descriptions. Employees were reluctant to work outside their job descriptions because they perceived that there was no mechanism to reward them. By combining individual salary ranges into one large range encompassing far more jobs, the organization could deploy workers in more tasks and projects for which they were suited without compromising their salary growth potential.

However, the organization introducing broadbanding may face an expectation on the part of employees and managers that the entire—and now much wider—salary range is available to a greater degree than it actually is. Employees are typically very sensitive to communication that salary growth has been greatly increased followed by salary actions that show no such growth, or worse, show such growth only for a very few individuals. Organizations expecting salary containment through broadbanding may wish they had selected another compensation arrangement. In fact, Martocchio says that the federal government experiences with broadbanding showed an increase in salary growth over traditional pay structures.[1] Fay et al. analyzed base salaries and total cash compensation for IT positions in service, manufacturing, high technology, nonprofit, and energy organizations for 2000 and 2001 to compare costs under broadbanding and under traditional salary ranges. (Nonprofit included government and education as well as nonprofit organizations.) The compensation costs for those positions, both base salaries and total cash compensation, were higher under broadbanding than under traditional salary ranges.[2]

Further, employees may see their promotional opportunities limited by broadbanding because jobs and job levels may have disappeared.

COMMISSION-BASED SALARY STRUCTURES

The commission compensation structure is typically assigned to sales people who receive a portion of the sales income generated by their efforts. These sales people may receive a salary as well, or a draw against future commissions, to provide some income stability. A commission structure assumes that the employee is self-directed and has the latitude to work harder and in whatever manner is most likely to achieve results. Typically, the job involves greater personal freedom and the results achieved can be measured in an unequivocal manner.

The commission pay structure is unlikely to be useful in government environments, although a commission structure has been used effectively in a healthcare setting when university medical faculty received a portion of the payments made by (or on behalf of) each patient. However, many services provided in a government setting do not result in direct revenue per transaction. In fact, it may cost money rather than bring in money to serve the public. Organizations that engage in fundraising may be in a position to place jobs engaged in the fundraising effort on a commission-type basis. Presumably, employees charged with fundraising will be more creative and industrious knowing that at least part of the money raised will find its way into their own financial accounts.

Unfortunately, donors may not see such an arrangement as a positive factor. Donors may not want to see themselves as the targets of a well-planned and energetic campaign implemented by those who will benefit from the resulting donations even before the organization and its clients do. Donors may even place constraints on how their donations are used to preclude a commission being paid from any funds they may choose to provide.

The prudent compensation manager must be very careful about implementing a commission-type structure for any jobs in the organization. The public relationship implications of such arrangements, if not handled very carefully and at the proper levels, could be quite troublesome.

SALARY RATES ESTABLISHED BY NEGOTIATION

Salary determination solely through individual negotiations is rarely considered a compensation structure, yet some version of this salary determination mechanism is inherent in many recruitments even in the public and nonprofit sectors. Certainly, the recruitment for a new top executive in the organization will proceed without regard to salary ranges if the governing board so decrees. Public agencies may allow hiring managers to make job offers as long as the salary offered does not exceed a predetermined level in the range, such as the 25th percentile or the 50th percentile (the midpoint).

One could make a case that salary rates determined by negotiation can bring the organization's pay rates closer to the market over time because an applicant will normally accept a job only if the offered salary is at least as high as the current salary. If the organization really wants to bring salaries closer to the external labor market, salary-by-negotiation might be worthy of consideration.

VARIABLE PAY

Employees receive variable pay by achieving goals set for them as individuals, part of a team, or as a member of the organization. The pay thus earned is added to the base salary as a one-time payment. In order for such rewards to be effective motivators, the environment must be such that the performance is measurable and that the individual, team, or organization has a line of sight from the efforts made to the rewards received. (Lawler points out that publicly announced quantitative measures of performance are better received by employees than subjective measures, particularly unknown subjective measures, which employees suspect of bias and inaccuracy.[3])

The compensation manager must consider whether variable pay is appropriate for each job or employee group/jobs combination. Do incumbents in the job have sufficient control over the resources available to them to achieve the objectives through their own or the group's industriousness and creativity? Most importantly, would the amount of the awards have to be budgeted in advance through the usual budgetary process, implying that the organization had determined in advance the objectives that would be reached in the coming year, by how many employees, and what those accomplishments would be worth? This latter point can be especially troublesome if the organization's salary increase budget requires approval by a legislative group, a religious order, or some other authority with a philosophical bias against "unnecessary" compensation. Such authorities may imply or say outright that of course these employees should achieve their objectives; such achievement means continued employment.

Therefore, the usefulness of variable pay for any particular job is directly related to multiple factors including:

- The degree of autonomy in the job.
- The degree to which performance is observable and measurable.
- The impact of performance in the job on organizational revenue.
- The attitude of the governing authority toward variable pay.

THE EXTERNAL LABOR MARKET

At some point, the compensation manager must come to grips with the salary survey issue and decide how to treat the external labor market. If an internal or external authority requires salary surveys according to some methodology and expects published results as part of the budgetary approval process, then at least part of that decision has been made for you. The budget process may incorporate the results of that survey in some sort of routine, formal way with little or no impact on the compensation structure itself. If, however, you are left on your own to determine the relationship between the external labor market and your revised or new compensation structure, then you will want to draw on the previous organizational and revenue analysis as part of that decision-making process.

Even if you never publicly articulate answers to the following questions, you will want to become comfortable with those answers:

- Is there an unspoken (or even spoken) belief within the electorate, the governing board, the legislature, or some other internal or external authority that salaries in your organization should always lag the market?
- Would your organization be willing to freeze salaries until it could no longer recruit or retain before implementing a salary increase?
- Does your organization believe, possibly with good reason, that there are no comparable institutions and that salary surveys are meaningless?
- Are you beginning your tenure as a compensation manager with existing salary levels so far below market that the results of a comparison to the external labor market are generally known at all levels of the organization and need not be reexamined?
- Were you brought into the organization to implement a way to remedy the salary gap between the organization and the external labor market?

The compensation manager has little choice but to complete any regular salary survey requirements according to the accepted methodology, if there is one. The less obvious responsibility is addressing the results. The prudent compensation manager may choose to be guided by the internal climate and organizational priorities at the time the external labor market survey is completed.

CONSTRUCTING SALARY RANGES

Before tackling the calculations required to construct salary ranges, the compensation manager should address the following issues according to the organization's priorities, the jobs to be included in each salary range, the applicability of any labor union contracts, the results of communication with internal and external authorities, and any other factors relevant to the organization in its current frame of reference. These issues include but are not limited to:

- How many salary ranges are appropriate for the workforce? *(Note: The format of the spreadsheet NewCOMP, shown at the end of this chapter, allows a salary range to encompass part of a single employee group, all of the employee group, or more than one employee group.)*
- Are there existing salary ranges for any of the employee group/jobs combinations?
- Which employee groups or jobs are to be included in each range?
- How wide should each salary range be? The rule of thumb is that the range spread for higher level jobs is significantly greater than the range spread for lower level jobs.
- Will any of the salary ranges be subdivided into steps?
- What kind of midpoint progression is considered suitable for the organization, if any?
- How will the organization handle current salaries for existing employees that are either above the maximum or below the minimum of a newly constructed salary range?

These are not the only questions to be asked in any particular organization, but they are central to the development of the new salary ranges.

If there is already a salary range for an identified employee group/jobs combination, how does it fit with the criteria previously described? If an existing salary range is in harmony with the answers to the preceding questions, then you may be able to simply transfer that existing salary range to the new or revised compensation structure.

Assuming that the salary range requires revision, the compensation manager will need to make tests similar to those used by Goldilocks: Is the range too high, too low, or just right? Is the range spread too wide, too narrow, or just right?

If there are existing incumbents for any or all of the jobs in the new salary range, the compensation manager might want to begin by calculating the average salary for all incumbents in those jobs, calling that average salary the midpoint, and then building a salary range around the midpoint with the desired range spread, as follows:

Assume that the average salary for all incumbents to be included in the salary range is $40,000. *Therefore, the midpoint of the new salary range is $40,000.*

Assume that the desired range spread is *50 percent, or .50 when expressed as a decimal.*

Calculate the range minimum

$$\text{Range minimum} = \frac{\text{Midpoint}}{1.0 + (\text{one-half of the total range spread expressed as a decimal})}$$

Sample:

$$\frac{\$40,000}{1.0 + .25} = \frac{\$40,000}{1.25} = \$32,000$$

Calculate the range maximum

$$\text{Range maximum} = \text{Range minimum} \times (1.0 + \text{Range spread expressed as a decimal})$$

Sample:

$$= \$32,000 \times 1.5 = \$48,000$$

New salary range

Minimum	$32,000
Midpoint	$40,000
Maximum	$48,000

Sometimes organizational factors "encourage" a compensation manager to place the top executive in a salary range to be shared with no other jobs. If so, the compensation manager may well be similarly encouraged to build that particular salary range in a specific manner. Unless there is some inherent reason why the specified salary range for the top executive would wreak havoc on the rest of the new compensation structure, it is probably wise to simply accept the arrangement and move on.

Once all the ranges have been created and assigned to the appropriate employee group/jobs combinations, the compensation manager can assess their interrelation and make whatever adjustments are necessary for desired midpoint progression, range overlap, and other factors. There are several reference books describing such calculations including Joseph J. Martocchio's *Strategic Compensation: A Human Resource Management Approach.*[1]

ADJUSTING FLAT RATES

Under the new or revised compensation structure, the employee group/jobs combinations to be paid at a flat rate are either already being paid at a flat rate or they are not. If incumbents are not currently paid at a flat rate, then the compensation manager will be changing the method of payment and possibly the rate as well. When communicating this reality to those affected, the compensation manager should rely on very sound and hopefully persuasive reasoning. Here is one possible scenario:

Compensation Manager Addressing Employees

"In the past, your job has been paid at a rate set within a salary range. Salary growth for your job was enabled by your movement through the salary range based on performance. However, experience has shown that most incumbents are promoted so rapidly that the salary range is rarely used for salary growth purposes. Therefore, the organization has decided to set a flat rate for the following jobs (*name the jobs*) at the following salary rates (*name the rates*)."

This little scene is only a hypothetical example. You will be guided in similar communication by your own good judgment about how, when, and with what turn of phrase to inform the workforce about the new compensation structure. Ideally, sound and logical reasoning will carry the day when the compensation manager stands before various employee groups to describe and defend the new structure.

Spreadsheet 9 (NewCOMP) displayed at the end of the chapter is intended to contain the elements of the new or substantially revised compensation structure. Please consider this spreadsheet a sample only. You may need to add or delete columns or rows in order to represent your organization's new structure.

Exempt/Nonexempt

The rows on NewCOMP are divided between exempt and nonexempt employee groups and related jobs. Because I have assumed that no single employee group includes both exempt and nonexempt jobs, the row designators "Exempt" and "Nonexempt" do not appear on the spreadsheet NewCOMP. Some other assumption might serve your organization better.

Range Code

This column identifies the salary range applicable to the employee group as a whole, to a block of jobs within the employee group, or to more than one employee group. You may choose to identify your ranges by letters (A, B, C, etc.), roman numerals (I, II, III, etc.), Arabic numerals (1, 2 3, etc.), or by some other code.

Employee Group

This column now contains the customized employee groups that drive the new compensation structure and reflect the ideal employee groups for the jobs and any EEO issues present in the organization. This column may not look like the columns of the same name in the prior EXMPT, NONEX, and JOBS spreadsheets.

Jobs

This column shows the jobs within each employee group. In selecting the order in which the jobs appear, you may want to rely on the results of your job evaluation method and list the jobs from the highest to the lowest value to the organization. The NewCOMP spreadsheet format assumes that employee groups are also listed in order of organizational hierarchy, from highest to lowest.

NEW SALARY RANGE

Assuming that there is to be a salary range for any employee group/jobs combination, these three columns will show the range minimum, midpoint, and maximum salary levels. If these values are zero or blank, then the salary for that job is not placed in a salary range.

SPREAD PERCENTAGE

This column displays the range spread as a percentage (%). As previously illustrated, calculating the range minimum and maximum around a midpoint uses the range spread expressed as a decimal.

STEPS

This column shows the number of steps in the salary range applicable to that job. A blank or 0 entry indicates that there are no steps in the salary range or that there is no range at all.

FLAT RATE

If the job is paid at a flat rate, this column shows the dollar amount per hour. If the flat rate is not an hourly rate, then the dollar amount should be accompanied by an indicator for the appropriate time period, for example, monthly, annually, biweekly, other.

COMMISSION

If pay for the job is determined in whole or in part through a commission arrangement, this column should contain the description of the basis for the commission. If the job is paid on commission plus a base salary, then there will be appropriate entries in another column indicating the nature of the base pay.

PERSON-BASED PAY

This column shows whether the job is eligible for person-based pay and if so, the basis for such pay. Possible bases for person-based pay include skills (lower level jobs), knowledge (often appropriate for exempt jobs), and competencies (management jobs). Other bases may be appropriate for your organization.

VARIABLE PAY

This column shows whether the job is eligible for variable pay and, if so, the basis for such pay. Options include attainment of goals and objectives set for the individual, a team, and for the entire organization.

BENCHMARK

This column identifies a job as a benchmark job or else identifies another job to which this job is linked for benchmarking. If the organization routinely uses one or more surveys or a set of comparison institutions for comparison data, that information should appear in this column.

PRIMARY INFLUENCE

The contents of this column may be the most important documentation retained by the compensation manager in developing the new or substantially revised compensation system. Unlike benchmarking (a formal process resulting in a structural job designation), Primary Influence describes one compensation manager's opinion of the true state of current organizational decision making: What really influences the salary rate for this job?
   Possible answers include:

- Salary increase budgets at other comparable institutions.
- National Consumer Price Index: current rate compared to the rate for some previous time period.
- Relationship between this job rate and the midpoint of the next highest range.

- Relationship between the incumbent's initial hire salary, the number of years of service, and the average salary budget increases for each of those years.
- Union Contract(s).
- Other.

This column contains your most candid assessment of the true basis underlying salary rate determination for each job.

Hopefully, preparing the seven previous spreadsheets coupled with your own professional awareness will make completing this column the embodiment of your understanding of this organization, its workforce, and the new compensation structure that ties them together.

NOTES

1. *Strategic Compensation: A Human Resource Management Approach,* Joseph J. Martocchio, 2001, Upper Saddle River, NJ: Prentice-Hall, p. 218.
2. "Broadbanding, Pay Ranges and Labor Costs," Charles Fay, PH.D., CCP; Eric Schulz; Steven E Gross; and David Van De Voort, CCP, *WorldatWork Journal,* 2004, vol. 13, no. 2, pp. 15–18.
3. *Rewarding Excellence: Pay Strategies for the New Economy,* Edward E. Lawler III, 2000, San Francisco, CA: Jossey Bass, p. 45.

SPREADSHEET 9   ABC COMMUNITY SERVICES—
NEW COMPENSATION STRUCTURE

Mission Statement: Provide Service to Those in Need

				New Salary Range				
	Range Code	Employee Group	Jobs	Minimum	Middle	Maximum	Spread Percent	Steps
Exempt		Senior management	Job 1					
			Job 2					
		Middle management	Job 1					
			Job 2					
		Professional	Job 1					
			Job 2					
		Other exempt	Job 1					
			Job 2					
		Confidential	Job 1					
			Job 2					
Nonexempt		Administrative	Job A					
			Job B					
		Skilled crafts	Job A					
			Job B					
		Laborers	Job A					
			Job B					
		Other unionized	Job A					
			Job B					

Sheet tabs: ORG / GOV / REV / WRKFRC / COMP / EXMPT / NONEX / JOBS / **NewCOMP** / PerfMgt / MAINT

Legend:

Range Code: A code identifying the salary range that sets the minimum and maximum salary rates for jobs within the range.

Employee Group: Broad groupings of employees based on jobs of similar type and scope. This column reflects any revisions to the employee groups, including revisions intended to address any EEO issues, and the employee groups shown here may differ from the employee groups shown on the WRKFRC and other previous spreadsheets.

Jobs: A set of duties performed by one or more incumbents. The job may be vacant but under recruitment.

New Salary Range: The minimum, midpoint, and maximum salary levels for a new salary range. If blank or 0, this particular job is not compensated according to a salary range.

Spread Percent: The difference between the maximum and minimum rates divided by the minimum rate and expressed as a percentage.

Steps: The number of steps in the range. A blank or 0 entry would indicate that there are no steps.

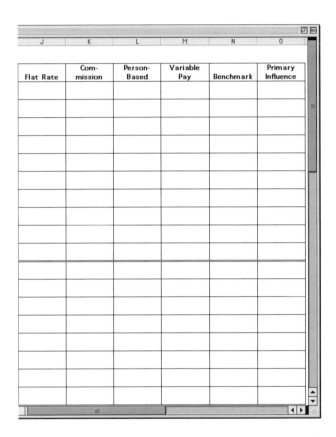

Flat Rate	Com- mission	Person- Based	Variable Pay	Benchmark	Primary Influence

Flat Rate: A single hourly rate at which all incumbents in the job are paid. If the rate is other than hourly, the column should show the rate and the applicable time period, for example, monthly, annual, other.

Commission: An arrangement by which incumbents in the job receive some portion of the revenue attributed to their efforts.

Person-Based Pay: Pay based on skills, knowledge, and/or competency acquired by the incumbents in this job.

Variable Pay: The basis of any variable pay that may be earned by incumbents in this job—for example, individual, team-based, or organizational.

Benchmark: The relationship of this job to the external labor market, either as a benchmark or linked to another job used as a benchmark.

Primary Influence: The entity, statistic, mechanism, comparison, or other influence that has the dominant effect on compensation for this job.

CHAPTER 10

Performance Management— Pay for Performance or Pay for Promotions?

If job analysis is the linchpin of human resources, performance management is its Achilles' heel. Any compensation manager is acquainted with the terms *performance management*, *performance appraisal*, *performance evaluation*, and perhaps other related terms. This book uses *performance evaluation* and *performance appraisal* interchangeably to mean the evaluation of past performance, usually within a specific time period. Performance management, the broader term, includes performance appraisal/evaluation as well as future actions to be taken by both the employee and the organization. Normally, these future actions concentrate on meeting future goals and standards as well as correcting any shortcomings noticed in the past review period and may address training needs and other career development issues. On the corrective side, the future actions can include progressive discipline based on poor performance, on-the-job behavior, or some other attribute.

Lawler, focusing primarily on the for-profit environment, notes the wide variation in pay levels for individuals in professional sports and entertainment where top performers make many times the salaries paid to the lesser performers.[1] This variation reflects the top performers' ability to attract fans and audiences to the various performances and the revenue associated with that ability. In traditional jobs, however, superb performance may add little more value to the organization than simply adequate performance. The following sections speak to limitation in pay-for-performance unique to the nonprofit and public organizations. The compensation manager may want to give serious thought to the value added by superior performance in each job. Further, the compensation manager may want to consider the importance of functional excellence in the overall performance of the organization.

Performance management requires revisiting the underlying reality of many public or nonprofit organizations: *outstanding performance by the organization, the team, and/or the individual may have only a marginal impact—or no impact—on revenue in the current time period or in the next.* If there is only a fragile connection between performance at any level and organizational revenue, then why would the organization pay for performance? What would the organization use to pay for performance since the excellence of performance does not result in a burst of revenue? Similarly, if internal or external authorities have predetermined the level of salary increase budgets regardless of revenue realities or expectations, how *can* the organization pay for performance?

By way of comparison, let's take that quintessential for-profit establishment we all know: the car dealership. What do you think happens to revenue for the car dealership under the following set of circumstances?

- The sales people sell every car that comes in to the lot in half the time normally needed to make such sales.
- The fleet manager keeps inventory at an ideal level, not too many cars but not too few.
- The finance manager qualifies all potential car buyers with unerring accuracy and lets no car go to a buyer with an unworthy credit history.
- The service department gets awards and local publicity for unfailing courtesy, prompt turnaround, and reasonable maintenance prices.
- The accounting staff monitors all expenditures closely, ensuring that the operation is fully supported, all bills paid in a timely fashion, and not one penny is wasted.

Do you think that this car dealership will be financially successful? Barring a terrorist attack or an act of God, this car dealership should be in an excellent position to pay for performance because the performance has already paid for itself.

Your Performance Management Mission

The broad term compensation *system* used in this book includes, in addition to the compensation structure, related areas such as performance management, the budget process, and Human Resource Information Systems (HRIS). Chapters 1 and 2 in this book addressed some of these issues.

This chapter addresses performance management which, if not part of the compensation structure, is certainly part of the broader compensation system. *The assessment of an incumbent's performance in a specific job and the subsequent organizational actions taken on the basis of that assessment mean a great deal to the employee.* Performance management may be the employee's bottom line.

If your organization has burdened you with overhauling the performance management process or developing such a process where none has existed before, this burden is going to test you on a number of fronts. Your success will depend on your understanding of the organization, your own professionalism, your sense of the possible, the resiliency of your network, and your remaining stock of good luck, to name a few factors. The following variables will shape your approach to tailoring a performance management process suitable to the organization and the newly developed compensation structure:

- Internal and external authorities
- Budget impact
- Organizational culture
- Supervisory attitudes
- Measurement basis

There may be additional variables unique to your organization and worthy of your attention. Spreadsheet 10 (PerfMgt) at the end of this chapter (and in Appendix B) is intended to document the desired approach to performance management given the new or substantially revised compensation structure.

Internal and External Authorities

Public agencies are subject to scrutiny by the electorate and typically follow a budget justification process to determine the salary increase budget for the coming year. This governmental budget request process addresses every component of the organization's budget, the salary increase piece being only one part among many. Those who bring the budget request forward and provide justification for each requested increase may not even mention organizational excellence as a justification for anything. Instead they may prefer to discuss unmet needs of the citizens the organization is mandated to serve. If excellence of organizational performance is deemphasized—or ignored—in the budget request process, it may be difficult for the organization to introduce pay for performance as an operational reality.

Worse, it is possible that superb performance could actually work to the organization's disadvantage. For example, if a fire department implements citywide fire prevention procedures so successfully that fires are reduced by 50 percent three years in a row, an external authority might reduce the fire department's budget because the public no longer "needs" that level of fire protection.

Nonprofit organizations focusing on such missions as healthcare, charity, religious worship, union membership, and members of specific professions, among others, may be closer to their clients and donors than public agencies are. The budget process may be internal rather than external, and there may be certain jobs that do bring in revenue in a manner reminiscent of a for-profit company. If the internal budget process is receptive to pay for performance, the organization certainly has more leeway to implement a more generous pay program.

However, nonprofit organizations with a strong philanthropic, religious, or service mission may have built-in inhibitions when it comes to awarding salary increases. These inhibitions may reflect the following issues:

- Unless the organization is very large with significant endowments, financial managers spend considerable effort in bringing *financial stability* into the organizations. Today's donations may not be repeated tomorrow, but salary commitments remain an ongoing burden. Reluctant to lay off workers, these organizations may seek to keep salary commitments as low as possible as a hedge against future diminished funds.

- If the organization has obtained contracts or grants and used these funds, at least in part, to pay employees, the *terms of the contracts and grants* may allow for a specific salary increase and no more, regardless of individual performance.

- Some of the funds received by the organization may *stipulate the purpose for which the funds can be used,* and this purpose may not include salaries or salary increases.

Previous chapters have referred to the revenue stream enjoyed by your organization and its limitations. You should keep these factors in mind when you fashion the performance management process.

Budget Impact

In most nonprofit and public environments, the employees are fully aware of the budgetary health of the organization. In many cases, the budget process is public knowledge and plays itself out in the newspapers and on television for weeks, if not months, every year. If there are union contracts that decree a certain salary increase, a publicly determined salary budget set by legislative approval, or some other generally known organizational controls that impact salary increases, the employees will know about them. If there is little or no money for salary increases, or if salary increases are controlled by some internal or external authority as to how they are administered, employees at all levels are fully aware of the situation. Mohrman, Resnick-West, and Lawler suggest that organizations with a minimal pay budget abandon any attempt to tie pay to performance if the result is minimal differences in salary increases between able and inadequate performers.[2]

No matter how hard the organization tries to separate performance evaluations from the reward structure, employees are going to believe—or want to believe—that better performance leads to better rewards. Better rewards are commonly translated as higher salary increases. If that is not true, then what is the value of better performance? Here lies the rub. Even highly capable human resources professionals may try in vain to implement effective performance management processes in organizations with historically low salary increase budgets.

Why is it important that your organization have a performance management process? Why does the organization believe that it is important? Would a competent compensation manager, knowing what you now know about the organization, recommend a performance management process? If so, what form would such a process take and how would it interact with the budgetary process?

Here are four reasons why an organization with little or no capability to award significant salary increases might want an effective performance management process:

1. To meet a requirement by an internal or external authority demanding that such a process be formally observed even in years with no salary increase budget.
2. To justify a promotion or upward reclassification.
3. To build a history of each employee's performance in case of layoff or termination for cause.
4. To document poor performance to pave the way to combat a grievance or litigation.

ORGANIZATIONAL CULTURE

By now, you may have spent a year or more meeting with people at all levels in your organization, researching the organization's past, and developing a new compensation structure. You may need little or no additional conversation and research to unearth the aspects of organizational culture that would impact performance management. However, you may want to pursue certain aspects of organizational attitudes toward assessing employee performance even further.

Important aspects of the organizational climate might include:

- Unspoken acceptance that the organization cannot pay external labor market rates and therefore has no right to expect superior performance.
- Emphasis on collegiality and a deemphasis on the role of the managerial hierarchy.
- Organizational unwillingness to pay supervisors significantly more than those they supervise in recognition of the supervisory burden.
- Emphasis on "catching people doing something right" rather than on correcting shortcomings.
- A lengthy termination process allowing the targeted employee to cause great damage to the organization before the termination takes place.
- Belief that job stability is part of the compensation offered by the organization.
- Belief that supervisors should continually monitor employee performance and provide feedback, making an annual review unnecessary.

- Fear that a positive performance evaluation might encourage the incumbent to request some sort of improvement in compensation beyond the capability of the organization.

- Belief that performance evaluations and rewards are separate and essentially unrelated events, making the evaluation nice to have but unrelated to salary administration.

- Fear on the part of management that litigation will result if a negative evaluation is given to an incumbent.

- Fear on the part of employees that performance reviews are done only as part of progressive discipline (perhaps justified by past practice).

- Confusion over how to construct a logical and documented performance evaluation, whether positive or negative.

- Fear of hurt feelings and loss of workforce morale.

These are only some of the factors that could discourage performance management in the organization.

One might say that all employees, represented or unrepresented, should receive regular performance evaluations, have the opportunity to give their opinions about their jobs and their performance in those jobs, and receive managerial feedback. Such an organizational belief may be the best reason of all for implementing a performance management process and has little or nothing to do with a compensation structure.

SUPERVISORY ATTITUDES

This area is probably the most delicate and potentially troublesome of all. Even HR executives charged with developing performance management policies may be less than rigorous about reviewing their own staff members. Many supervisors look askance at performance evaluations, and with good reasons. Some of those reasons include:

- Supervisors may believe that an annual performance evaluation is useless. If the result of the evaluation is negative, the employee will retaliate by saying that the supervisor waited a year to say that there was a problem. The employee may then allege discrimination, harassment, or some other infraction and tie up the supervisor for a year, to say nothing of litigation. If the employee wins, other employees will mark down that technique for successfully rebutting a negative evaluation.

- Supervisors believe that they can't win even if there is no employee retaliation. With limited or predetermined salary increase budgets, those employees with excellent performance evaluations will be resentful because there are no commensurate rewards, and those with negative evaluations will be angry because of the evaluation content. Those with average evaluations will be indifferent, and no one will be pleased.
- Supervisors may distrust senior management and believe that executives have already decided which employees are good performers. Evaluations to the contrary will be ignored by those senior managers.
- Supervisors believe that the grievance processes for either represented or unrepresented employees, or both, are such that their performance evaluations can be overturned.

Few factors can cripple a well-thought-out performance management process like the refusal of supervisors to implement the system.

Although it is possible for a compensation manager to devise a compensation structure without too much involvement with other managers, the development of a performance management process is much more of a group effort. If the supervisors resist your ideas for a performance evaluation process, you must amend your ideas until they accept them or you run out of ideas. In the latter case, you have little choice but to tell those who charged you with this responsibility that you have been unable to reach agreement with those whose cooperation is essential.

It is possible that the performance management process you are to devise is cosmetic in nature. It must exist in policy, but the organization will honor it in the breach without too much discomfort. While such a project is not very satisfying, at least the compensation manager can complete the project and implement it to whatever degree possible.

MEASUREMENT BASIS

Putting organizational culture and attitudinal issues aside, a compensation manager establishing a performance management process must address the appropriate basis for measuring performance. Mohrman, Resnick-West, and Lawler identify four separate measurement bases:[3]

1. Performer-oriented: traits and skills
2. Behavior-oriented: critical incidents, predetermined

3. Results-oriented

4. Comparison-oriented: employee to employee

Plachy and Plachy focus on results rather than on behaviors on the belief that job results can be evaluated with respect to the organization's mission.[4] Whether the compensation manager selects job results, one of the other three approaches previously listed, or some other basis, there may remain a disconnect between performance that furthers the organization's *mission* and performance that furthers the organization's *revenue*.

THE IMPORTANCE OF PROMOTIONS

Many public and nonprofit organizations are severely limited in their ability to reward an employee whose performance has been stellar. Either the salary range for the position is limited, or the employee is at or near the top of the applicable range, or the employee is paid at a flat rate, or worse, the employee has had the bad luck to perform superbly in a year with little or no salary increase budget. In any of these cases, the organization may be left with only one option to reward the employee and yet stay within the financial constraints: promotion.

By "promotion," I am also including an upward reclassification. In the former, the employee changes jobs and is now in a higher level job. In the latter, a job analysis determines that the employee is actually already doing the tasks associated with a higher level position. In either case, the employee may be eligible for two kinds of salary increase:

1. General increase, assuming that a general salary increase has been approved for that year.

2. Promotional/reclassification increase used only when such personnel actions occur.

When added together, the two increases may be two or more times the general increase. Because promotions and reclassifications occur with far less frequency, the budgetary burden may be minimal. One of the questions on the survey (Appendix A) asked how an employee could, by individual effort, increase his or her salary. Based on more than one response to that question, the best single answer is "Get promoted."

The spreadsheet PerfMgt at the end of this chapter is technical in nature and should be consistent with the organizational factors discussed so far in this chapter.

EMPLOYEE GROUP

These employee groups are those assigned in the new compensation structure and reflect employees whose jobs have common characteristics.

JOBS

These are the jobs identified in the new compensation structure and may be listed in order of value to the organization as determined by the job analysis process.

REVENUE IMPACT

This field reflects the degree to which performance in the job is directly related to the organization's revenue stream.

PERFORMANCE REVIEW SCHEDULE

This schedule describes the timing of the performance appraisals in the new or proposed performance management process. Options include but are not limited to:

- Annually on the employee's anniversary hire date
- Annually at the end of the calendar or budget year
- Periodically, for example, quarterly or semiannually
- Whenever the employee demonstrates exceptional performance, either good or bad

SALARY INCREASE SCHEDULE

This field records the date(s) or time periods on which salary increases become effective. The budgetary process determines this date. If the performance management process is supposed to be as separate as possible from the salary increase determination, then it might be useful to keep the performance review schedule and the salary increase schedule on a very different timetable.

COMPENSATION ARRANGEMENT

This field reflects the compensation arrangement of the job under the new compensation structure. Options include a flat rate, salary range with or without steps, variable pay tied to individual or team objectives, or person-based pay.

BASE SALARY INCREASE

This field records the relationship between the performance management process and an increase to the base salary. The compensation manager would want to address base-building and non-base-building salary increases in this column.

VARIABLE PAY

This field records the nature of any variable pay for which incumbents in the job are eligible. Variable pay can be based on individual, team, or over-all organization performance, at least in theory.

MEASUREMENT BASIS

Options include performer-oriented, behavior-oriented, results-oriented, comparison-oriented, and other.

PERFORMANCE REVIEW TECHNIQUE

This shows the methods by which performance in the job is assessed. Methods include BARS, graphic rating, essay, 360-degree, and other assessment techniques.

NOTES

1. *Rewarding Excellence: Pay Strategies for the New Economy,* Edward E. Lawler III, 2000, San Francisco, CA: Jossey-Bass, pp. 4–6.
2. *Designing Performance Appraisal Systems: Aligning Appraisals and Organizational Realities,* Allan M. Mohrman, Jr., Susan M. Resnick-West, Edward E. Lawler III, 1989, San Francisco, CA: Jossey-Bass, p. 178.
3. Ibid., p. 50.
4. *Building a Fair Pay Program: A Step-by-Step Guide,* 2nd Edition, Roger J. Plachy and Sandra J. Plachy, 1998, New York: AMACOM (American Management Association), pp. xv–xvi.

Mission Statement: Provide Service to Those in Need

	Employee Group	Jobs	Revenue Impact	Performance Review Schedule	Salary Increase Schedule
1					
2	Senior management	Job 1			
3		Job 2			
4	Middle management	Job 1			
5		Job 2			
6	Professional	Job 1			
7		Job 2			
8	Other exempt	Job 1			
9		Job 2			
10	Confidential	Job 1			
11		Job 2			
12	Administrative	Job A			
13		Job B			
14	Skilled crafts	Job A			
15		Job B			
16	Laborers	Job A			
17		Job B			
18	Other unionized	Job A			
19		Job B			

(Exempt: rows 2–11; Nonexempt: rows 12–19)

Tabs: ORG / GOV / REV / WRKFRC / COMP / EXMPT / NONEX / JOBS / NewCOMP / **PerfMgt** / MAINT

Legend:

Employee Group: Broad groupings of employees based on jobs of similar type and scope. This column reflects any revisions to the employee groups, including revisions intended to address any EEO issues, and the employee groups shown here may differ from the employee groups shown on the WRKFRC and other previous spreadsheets.

Jobs: A set of duties performed by one or more incumbents. The job may be vacant but under recruitment.

Revenue Impact: How does performance in the job affect revenue?

Performance Review Schedule: The timing of performance reviews for incumbent(s) in the job.

Salary Increase Schedule: The timing of the effective date of salary increases for incumbents in the job.

Compensation Arrangement	Base Salary Increase	Variable Pay	Measurement Basis	Performance Review Technique

Compensation Arrangement: The nature of the compensation applicable to this job under the new structure, for example, ranges with or without steps, flat rates, commissions, variable pay, other.

Base Salary Increase: The relationship between base salary increases and the performance management process.

Variable Pay: Type(s) of variable pay for which incumbent(s) in the job are eligible.

Measurement Basis: Performer-oriented, behavior-oriented, results-oriented, comparison-oriented, other.

Performance Review Technique: List the performance review technique(s) for the job such as BARS, graphic rating, essay, 360-degree, other.

CHAPTER **11**

Maintenance—Is It That Time Already?

During the development and implementation of a new or substantially revised compensation structure, maintenance of the new structure may have seemed far in the future. However, the need to make changes to the new structure may surface shortly after its implementation, leaving the organization and the compensation manager gasping for breath.

Managers and staff are already familiar with compensation changes triggered by the annual salary increase cycle. After all, the organization has paid its employees and increased their pay from time to time whether it had a formal compensation structure or not. The difference between changes to employee pay and changes to the compensation structure may be less clear. The compensation manager should emphasize to both colleagues and management that these two actions are separate in concept.

If all employees hold jobs that are compensated according to salary ranges, and none of those employees are paid at the maximum of their respective ranges, then each employee can receive some salary increase without a structural increase. In other words, the salary ranges can remain unchanged even though employee pay goes up. It is theoretically possible to give no salary increases to anyone and yet adjust the salary ranges upward as a provision for future salary growth in some future year.

However, some employees may be paid at a flat rate. If the contract mandates a 3 percent increase to that flat rate, then employee salaries will go up and that piece of the compensation structure will be revised upwards. Each type of pay increase and related compensation structure component has its own set of interrelationships.

In addition to structural changes related to the annual salary increase process, there are other reasons for revising the compensation structure sooner than anticipated. Such reasons include but are not limited to:

- Management has altered the responsibilities for one or more jobs indicating a need for job reanalysis and reevaluation.
- New jobs have been introduced into the workforce.
- Jobs have been deleted from the workforce.
- Jobs have been reassigned from one employee group to another employee group.
- Compensation arrangements for certain jobs have been revised due to perceived inequities, changes in the external labor market, union negotiations, pressure from employees, or managerial discretion.

There can be many other reasons, such as those related to a reorganization impacting multiple levels of jobs.

Once the compensation manager has identified the elements of the compensation structure requiring maintenance, another task may lie ahead: bringing about general acceptance of the need for compensation structure maintenance. Such acceptance may cross organizational unit boundary lines because of the burden imposed on other organizational units besides compensation and human resources. The payroll, information technology, and budget units, for example, may be prepared to increase individual pay rates promptly on request but be unsure how to respond to requests for maintaining the structure itself, or even whether they need to respond.

Adding jobs, deleting jobs, and increasing the salary ranges require such changes as revising the edit routines so that salary rates at the new maximum rate are not flagged by the payroll system as invalid. Each organization will have its own version of the information system changes needed to accommodate revisions to the compensation structure. Although maintaining the compensation structure is a high priority for the compensation manager, other organizational units may place such maintenance at the bottom of their priority list, or off the list altogether. In such cases, the compensation manager may need senior management to accept and support the maintenance effort by placing compensation structure maintenance in the priority list for each of the organizational units involved.

To reduce the burden of structure maintenance as much as possible, the compensation manager should devise routine, predictable procedures to address all foreseeable effort. Evaluating the external labor market through published and/or customized salary surveys is a compensation task commonly undertaken on a regular and predictable basis. The compensation manager may want to informally share this information with those units affected by a need to revise the compensation structure. This advance notice of possible future structural maintenance allows these organizations time to plan and devote sufficient resources to address compensation structure maintenance. The compensation structure maintenance effort is likely to involve accounting (payroll), other areas of human resources (policies and union agreements), the budget unit (position control), and information technology, especially if the organization runs its own payroll and related human resources information systems.

In the public and nonprofit environments, there can be a great deal of pressure on these organizational units to await the results of some action that will trigger their intense involvement, yet remain outside their control or influence. Some of the actions that could prove frustratingly slow in a public or nonprofit environment include:

- A budget process that goes on longer than expected.
- Union negotiations that await the results of the budget process.
- An audit by an external regulatory agency that could result in an equity adjustment to the compensation arrangements for various jobs.
- Statutory changes that might impact general human resources policies with implications for various jobs.
- Certification or decertification of one or more unions.

Coordinating a technical effort such as a change to a compensation structure requires the compensation manager to network effectively with colleagues, keeping them informed of the various possible changes to the compensation structure until the outcome is known.

Spreadsheet 11 (MAINT) at the end of this chapter (and in Appendix B) contains information that records any changes from the old structure to the new structure. The fields selected are those likely to be of use to an organization, and the flexibility of the spreadsheet software allows the compensation manager to add other fields. For example, the compensation manager might want to add dates on which changes were initiated for documentation purposes.

EMPLOYEE GROUP

A change to one or more employee groups is one of the most far-reaching changes to the compensation structure possible. Ideally, such major changes will be rare. Some hypothetical reasons why the information related to an employee group would change include:

- Employees decertify a union, nullifying the collective bargaining agreement and changing the applicable compensation arrangements. Those jobs are then merged into another employee group.

- Employees certify and elect a union, creating a new employee group whose members hold jobs compensated according to a new collective bargaining agreement.

- The organization revisits a job analysis and decides that jobs previously classified as exempt are actually nonexempt, or the other way around.

- The organization decides to have two separate managerial employee groups instead of one: one employee group for technical management and the other for general management.

- The organization decides to reorganize, reevaluates some jobs, and then reassigns those jobs to a lower employee group. However, rather than appear to demote existing employees, the organization grandfathers the employees in the reassigned jobs and continues to include those employees in the original employee group. Only new hires to the reassigned jobs will be placed in the lower level employee group.

- The organization eliminates a number of jobs and merges the employee group that used to include those jobs into another existing employee group.

Changes of this magnitude are likely to be accompanied by policy and procedural changes and may be motivated by external factors that affect the compensation structure but did not originate from the compensation manager.

The spreadsheet MAINT at the end of this chapter should display the new employee group/jobs combinations. The accounting and information technology units may need a crosswalk between the old and the new employee groups, especially if there are not only new employee groups but shifting of jobs from one to another.

Jobs

This column on the MAINT spreadsheet should contain every job that existed both in the previous compensation structure and will exist in the revised structure. As usual, each job represents a set of duties held by one or more employees or vacant but under recruitment. The viewer can quickly tell which jobs are deleted and which are new by looking at the next column, Status.

Status

This field shows for each job in both the old and new structure whether the job is new to the structure, just deleted from the structure, revised in some way, or in any other status the organization wishes to track. This spreadsheet, prepared each time the structure is maintained, provides a record of the evolution of the structure over time. Jobs deleted from the structure will make their final appearance on the MAINT spreadsheet.

Job Description

The organization can use this field to record whether changes were made to the job description and, if desired, indicate the type of changes made.

Job Evaluation

This column can indicate if the job was subject to reevaluation and related information, such as the evaluation method used and why, at the discretion of the compensation manager. The compensation manager may want to include information related to the job's former evaluation level.

Turnover

This column contains turnover statistics for each job calculated in whatever manner the compensation manager chooses to calculate that statistic. The viewer of the MAINT spreadsheet can simply scan the column to spot jobs with exceptionally high turnover rates and take action, if desired.

Compensation Arrangement

This column shows the compensation arrangement for each job under the new compensation structure. The compensation manager may want to modify the spreadsheet to include companion columns that have additional compensation arrangement information, such as background regarding the change and effective dates.

Impact

This field records the impact of any changes to the job and/or employee group on other units in the organization, information systems, and even external organizations such as unions, regulatory or certification agencies, governmental agencies, and donors. This field can serve as a record of those who must be involved in the implementation of a change to the compensation structure and the nature of that involvement. Additional columns could record deadlines for the involvement, if desired.

Management View

This column records any management decisions or needs to which the new structure responds. If the same management issue applies to multiple jobs or employee groups, the compensation manager can simply use the spread-sheet copy feature and quickly apply the same words to all the employee groups and/or jobs affected. This column may also be used to indicate de-cisions by external authorities, or the compensation manager may choose to add a column to the spreadsheet for that purpose.

SPREADSHEET II   ABC COMMUNITY SERVICES—
MAINTAINING THE STRUCTURE

Mission Statement: Provide Service to Those in Need

	Employee Group	Jobs	Status	Job Description
1	**Employee Group**	**Jobs**	**Status**	**Job Description**
2	Senior management	Job 1		
3		Job 2		
4	Middle management	Job 1		
5		Job 2		
6	Professional	Job 1		
7		Job 2		
8	Other exempt	Job 1		
9		Job 2		
10	Confidential	Job 1		
11		Job 2		
12	Administrative	Job A		
13		Job B		
14	Skilled crafts	Job A		
15		Job B		
16	Laborers	Job A		
17		Job B		
18	Other unionized	Job A		
19		Job B		

(Rows 2–11 labeled **Exempt**; rows 12–19 labeled **Nonexempt**)

Sheet tabs: ORG / GOV / REV / WRKFRC / COMP / EXMPT / NONEX / JOBS / NewCOMP / PerfMgt / **MAINT**

Nonprofit Spreadsheet.xls

Legend:

Employee Group: Broad groupings of employees based on jobs of similar type and scope. Any changes to the employee groups themselves as a result of structure maintenance would be shown in this column. Such changes are likely to be linked to other more general human resources changes.

Jobs: A set of duties performed by one or more incumbents. The job may be vacant but under recruitment.

Status: Is this job under revision, to be added, to be deleted, or in some other status?

Job Description: Does the job description for the job exist (if new) or need to be revised?

Job Evaluation: Does the job need to be reevaluated according to the selected job evaluation technique?

F	G	H Compensation Arrangement	I	J
Job Evaluation	Turnover		Impact	Management View

Turnover: Recruitment/retention statistics for the Job.

Compensation Arrangement: Is the compensation arrangement for the position changed as part of the maintenance effort and, if so, what is the new arrangement?

Impact: The automated systems and organizational units, including labor unions, that will be affected by the revision, if any, to this job.

Management View: Formal or informal feedback from management and/or the governing body regarding the job, the employee group, or the structure itself.

CHAPTER 12

Conclusion—The Bottom Line

Throughout this book I have tried to alert the reader to unique aspects of public and nonprofit environments that could impact the effort to substantially revise an existing compensation structure or devise a completely new one. The following list indicates four primary variables:

1. Nature of revenue
2. Relationship between organizational success and revenue
3. Pay for performance or promotion
4. Coordination within the organization

No doubt, these variables also exist in the for-profit world. However, their nature in the public or nonprofit environments may influence the compensation manager's efforts in a very different manner. The following discussion assumes that the reader's primary or sole professional experience has occurred in the for-profit world.

NATURE OF REVENUE

Members of the workforce earn money from their employment and, once earned, that money becomes theirs to do with as they wish within the bounds of legality and, it is to be hoped, common sense. Similarly, for-profit organizations provide goods and services to the public and use the resulting revenue to pay expenses, reinvest in the business, and pay any shareholder obligations, as the organization so chooses. In the case of some consumer goods such as appliances and cars, for example, the manufacturer or dealer may have no obligation beyond the transaction other than selling the item as advertised and abiding by whatever warranties apply.

Among public and nonprofit environments, incoming funds may be considered more custodial than earned. (We are all familiar with the old story about a taxpayer who tells a law enforcement officer, "Just remember, I pay your salary.") The taxpaying public rarely describes its tax payments to various levels of government as money "earned" by the government.

Similarly, donations to religious and charitable organizations take on a different context than payment for religious services provided or for numbers of needy individuals served. Public and nonprofit organizations may impose strict rules on employees concerning the acceptance of gifts or even a lunch from anyone with whom the organization might have financial dealings. The workforce in a public or nonprofit environment may be subtly or overtly pressured to exhibit motives other than compensation for working for the organization.

Funds coming into the public and nonprofit environments may be categorized by their potential use in the following manner: unrestricted, temporarily restricted, or permanently restricted. The organization can spend unrestricted funds on whatever it wishes. Temporarily restricted funds may be spent only in certain ways and possibly only at certain times. Permanently restricted funds, such as a donation or endowment, may not be spent at all. Instead, the donation becomes the principal and only the income resulting from the investment of the donation or endowment is available to be spent by the organization, and even that income may be temporarily restricted.

Put simply, in the for-profit organization, money once earned is then owned. Incoming money to the nonprofit or public organization may be so constrained as to its use that its relationship to "revenue" in the for-profit sense is fragile, indeed. The constraints on incoming funds impact the compensation arrangements that can be made realistically available for various jobs.

RELATIONSHIP BETWEEN ORGANIZATIONAL SUCCESS AND REVENUE

The mission of the nonprofit organization describes its operational focus. Administering these organizations involves a vision of what excellence in performance of its mission might be. Senior managers spend considerable effort in determining how close the reality of the organization's performance comes to that vision. Law enforcement, healthcare, a church or synagogue, education—all these organizations have ways of assessing their own performance relative to their ideals.

The revenue earned by these organizations, however, may not be tied closely to the excellence of the performance of the mission. For example, a law enforcement organization that reduces the crime rate, a school that improves student test scores by a measurable amount, a hospital that provides higher quality healthcare at less cost, a charity that stretches its donated dollars over more services for the needy—these organizations may receive even fewer funds in the coming year than they received in years when the organizational performance was less admirable. Performance in a public or nonprofit organization is related to revenue, but only marginally in the short term.

PAY FOR PERFORMANCE OR PROMOTION

An organization that experiences little or no revenue growth resulting from excellent performance may not provide fertile soil for a pay-for-performance program. In fact, public and some nonprofit organizations may be under considerable pressure to hold down salaries no matter what level of performance its employees exhibit.

Current pay-for-performance theory focuses on rewarding performance in the position held by the employee. However, public and nonprofit organizations may offer only minimal rewards for performance in the position, reserving greater rewards for those who perform so well in their current positions that they can move to other, higher level positions. One might describe this pay philosophy as pay for promotion rather than pay for performance.

In fairness, an organization that promotes its high performers and then pays a commensurate salary *is* following a pay-for-performance pay policy. After all, promotions are based on factors such as performance, or they should be. Also, promotions are less frequent and represent a lesser financial burden. Even an electorate or donor unwilling to accept pay for performance will agree that a higher level job should be paid more than a lower level job.

COORDINATION WITHIN THE ORGANIZATION

What organization does not tell its employees that they are all on the same team, every job is important, the workforce is the organization's greatest asset, and other similar remarks intended to build morale and camaraderie? The public or nonprofit organizations might say these things and mean them just as sincerely. However, teamwork may take a very different form in the public or nonprofit organization than in the for-profit organization.

The compensation manager charged with substantially revising or designing a new compensation structure must network with all levels of management in the organization, possibly even including the governing body, either internal or external. When any aspect of the new compensation structure imposes a burden on another organizational unit, such as payroll or information technology, the compensation manager may have to take the lead in seeking out his fellow managers from those areas and learning enough about the rhythm of the workload in those units to knowledgeably coordinate his or her need for their assistance. This unspoken requirement to learn a good deal about the work of other units as part of the compensation manager's *own* work may be unique to the public and nonprofit environments.

Back to Baseball

The newly savvy expatriate/compensation manager has learned to watch the game carefully before taking up the bat and approaching the plate.

Do players choose when to swing, or do they swing at all the pitches?

Does the pitcher avoid the strike zone or aim for it with every pitch?

Does the team watch another point go up on the scoreboard with joy or gloom?

Wisely, the compensation manager/expatriate no longer assumes that his considerable experience and skill at a similar game will apply directly to this new version being played in a foreign land.

Now—batter up!

Survey—Compensation in Nonprofit/Public Organizations

Dear Survey Participant:

I want to thank you for agreeing to participate in the enclosed survey of compensation philosophy, structure, and management in nonprofit and public organizations. Your contribution to my research is invaluable to me and, I hope, to future readers.

I suspect that you will find this survey quite different from those you have designed or completed in the past. Frankly, I have never completed or designed a survey quite like this one, which addresses organizational assumptions, assessments, and practicality related to compensation.

For this research effort, I am far less interested in how much you pay employees than how and why you pay them as you do. Equally interesting, if not more so, are the compensation approaches and techniques your organization rejected—*and why*, the new techniques that you believe will or will not fit your organization—*and why*.

The enclosed survey begins with definitions of terms no doubt already familiar to you. In my own experience, familiar terms have a way of wandering around their original meanings until one finds that they have taken on another interpretation altogether. Therefore, I will ask you to complete this survey using the terms as defined, if at all possible. (I would be most interested in any alternative meanings you care to share.)

You may complete the survey in writing, electronically, or orally and return the results by mail, email, fax, or telephone in the case of an oral response. I hope that you will not mind a question or two later to make sure that I understand your responses and their context.

As is customary, your responses will be held in confidence and will not be separately identifiable.

Once again, I thank you for your time, trouble, and most of all, for the breadth and depth of your experience.

Sincerely,

JoAnn Senger

Enclosure

DEFINITIONS

Term	*Definition*
Budget	The timing and periodicity of the organization's revenue stream. For example, a government agency may receive a budget once a year and be required legally to keep expenditures within those limits. Other nonprofit organizations may struggle to estimate revenue and to cope with an unpredictable revenue stream.
Budget process	The activities necessary to raise funds and/or justify a budget request, estimate revenue, and plan expenditures within the budget once it is known; the timeframe and periodicity of the process; and the determination of the amount of funds to be used for salary increases.
Employer	An organization that pays employees on a regular schedule through a payroll process. The organization may or may not use independent contractors or volunteers in addition to employees to accomplish its mission.
Governing body	A board of directors, regents, trustees, the electorate, to name a few.
Job analysis	The process through which the organization analyzes a related set of activities or responsibilities and derives job descriptions and job specifications.
Job evaluation	The technique used by the employer to determine the relative value of jobs: • *Whole job:* A collection of job content evaluation techniques that compare jobs with each other or against general criteria. • *Classification plan:* A whole job evaluation technique that places jobs into predetermined categories, or classes, on the basis of class descriptions or benchmark jobs.

Term	*Definition*
	• *Point method:* A quantitative job evaluation technique that assigns points to the compensable factors that describe jobs. These points are totaled for each job as an indicator of the overall value of that job. Base pay is then aligned with market rates for benchmark jobs.
	• *Factor comparison:* A technique that begins with the selection of benchmark jobs, the selection of compensable factors, and ranking all the benchmark jobs factor by factor.
Nonprofit employer	An employer that may or may not serve its clientele or sell its services for more than the costs involved (i.e., earn a profit). If the employer does earn a profit, that profit is returned to the organization. The organization does not pay income taxes on revenue earned through its primary mission. *Note:* For purposes of this survey, this definition includes both private nonprofit organizations and government agencies.
Pay grade	A pay policy that applies to a group of jobs of similar worth.
Performance management	The process by which an organization communicates to employees what is expected of them, monitors their accomplishments, and responds with appropriate rewards, learning opportunities, and/or corrective actions.
Bases for salary increases	The behavior or job outcome rewarded by the organization through its compensation structure:
	• *Merit:* Base pay increase according to a performance evaluation.
	• *Seniority:* Base pay increase according to the employee's length of service in the job.

Term	*Definition*

- *Longevity:* Base pay increases awarded to employees who are at their pay grade maximum and not likely to move into higher pay grades.

- *Incentive (or variable) pay:* Compensation, other than base wages or salaries, that fluctuates according to the attainment of some standard, for example, a preestablished formula such as a commission plan, individual or group goals, or organization-wide revenue.

- *Person-based pay:* Increase in base pay because the employee acquires additional skills (physical worker), knowledge (professional worker), or competencies (manager).

ORGANIZATIONAL PROFILE

The following questions address your organization and its frame of reference relevant to compensation.

Type of Nonprofit/Public:_____
(Possible answers include religious, charity, municipal agency, school district, foundation, or other types of organizations.)

Mission: _____

_____

_____

Number of Employees:

	Full-Time Employees	Part-Time Employees
Exempt		
Management/Supervisory		
Other Exempt		
Nonexempt		

How many employees are represented through collective bargaining agreements? _____

What is the percentage of nonexempt employees represented through collective bargaining agreements?_____

Please list the unions that represent various employees:

_____

_____

_____

_____

BUDGET

Describe briefly your organization's revenue flow. You may include fundraising, any formal or informal budget justification to internal units/governing bodies/external agencies, predictability, controllability, timing, and any other factors that could influence compensation decision making.

Does your organization engage in fundraising?

Yes ___ No ___

If yes, please describe.

- Permanent fundraising staff
- Regular fundraising efforts
- Ad hoc fundraising efforts
- Other

If your organization engages in fundraising, what is the effect of fundraising on the budget planning process? For example, the manager of fundraising might be involved in all budget meetings.

How does organizational success with respect to the organization's mission impact fundraising or budget justification efforts? In other words, does operational success bring in greater revenue?

Describe briefly your process for allocating funds for salary increases.

How does the external labor market influence the amount of your organization's salary increase budget?

GOVERNANCE

Describe your organization's governing body. (One possible answer: a seven-person board of directors serving two-year terms, staggered.)

Does this governing body include employee representatives as ex officio, appointed, or elected?

Yes ___ No ___

If yes, please describe.

How does the governing body impact compensation decisions? Possible answers could include:

- review compensation structure annually and recommend changes.
- approve all individual salaries.
- approve senior management salaries only.
- approve salary increase budget.
- other.

If your organization's compensation structure is determined, either directly or indirectly, by the voting public, please describe how the voters exercise that influence. For example, the salary increase amount or percentage requires legislative approval.

JOB EVALUATION

Does your organization have a formal job evaluation process?

Yes ___ No ___
If yes, please describe.

What role does the market play in your job evaluation process? For example, your organization might tie the internal relative worth of jobs to the local external labor market in some way.

Please identify the group(s) of employees associated with the following job evaluation methods.

Whole Job:

Classification:

Point Method:

Factor Comparison:

Other:

Why has your organization elected to use the job evaluation method(s) you indicate above?

PAY STRUCTURES

Please describe the pay structures your organization uses and the employee groups to which they apply:

BASE SALARY

Ranges with steps:

Open ranges (a maximum and a minimum but no steps):

Broad band:

Flat rate:

Other:

VARIABLE PAY

None:

Yes:

- Individual incentive pay
- Team-based
- Organization-wide

INITIAL PAY AT TIME OF HIRE

Set by individual negotiation:

Hiring ranges within each structure (may include reference to the range midpoint):

Degree of compensation flexibility for hiring manager:

REWARDS

Please select the various salary increase drivers used by your organization. Also indicate the employee groups to which they apply.

BASE SALARY INCREASES

Merit:

General increase/COLA:

Seniority:

Longevity:

INCENTIVE (VARIABLE) PAY INCREASES

Individual:

Team:

Organization-wide:

PERSON-BASED PAY

Skills-based:

Knowledge-based:

Competency:

TYPE OF REWARD

Percent increase to base salary:

Nonbase building (temporary increase to base salary):

Lump sum:

Other:

TIMING

Annual:

Anniversary:

Budget cycle:

Other:

PERQUISITES

Does your organization have the flexibility to award perquisites to an employee such as a health club membership, car allowance, or other?

Yes ___ No ___

If yes, please describe the perquisites which may be awarded.

Describe the organizational factors that permit or prevent awarding such perquisites.

Performance Management

Does your organization have a formal performance management process for one or more employee groups?

Yes ___ No ___

If so, please identify each group and the related process in general terms.

How do employees find out about their salary increases?

How do the performance management process (if any) and the salary increase determination process interact in your organization?

How can an employee in your organization significantly impact his/her compensation through his/her performance?

BENEFITS

Please describe in general terms the various benefits offered by your organization and the employee groups to which they apply:

Medical:

Dental:

Vision:

Other health-related benefits:

Pension plan:

Supplementary retirement (401k, 403b, other):

Paid time off:

Other benefits:

Do you believe that the health benefits offered by your organization to all or most employees exceed the benefits they would enjoy in most for-profit employers?

Yes ___ No ___

If yes, please say why.

Do you believe that the pension/retirement benefits offered by your organization to all or most employees exceed the pension/retirement benefits they would enjoy in most for-profit employers?

Yes ___ No ___

If yes, please say why.

Do you believe that employees in your organization enjoy greater job security than they would in the average for-profit employer?

Yes ___ No ___

If yes, please say why.

GENERAL QUESTIONS

How does your organization's mission affect your compensation structure and practices? For example, if your organization is a charity, the board of directors might be uneasy when approving staff salary increases, reasoning that donors want their donations to go to the needy, not to the staff.
Is there an incentive—budgetary and/or organizational—to consider compensation structures new to your organization?

Yes ___ No ___
If yes, please describe.

If your organization wanted to implement a bonus program, would funds have to be allocated for bonuses at the beginning of the budgetary year?

Yes ___ No ___
If yes, please describe how such an allocation for bonuses would be determined.
If no, please indicate how bonuses could be funded.

How would (or does) incentive (variable) pay fit with your organizational climate?

Complete Spreadsheet Workbook

SPREADSHEET 1   ABC COMMUNITY SERVICES— THE ORGANIZATION

Note: The mission statement is the most important piece of information on this worksheet and appears in the heading on all subsequent worksheets.

	Characteristic	Description
1	**Characteristic**	**Description**
2	Type of organization	Government / Nonprofit
3	Operational focus	For example, law enforcement, religious, education, charity, health care, other
4	**Mission statement**	**Brief description of the organization's contribution to constituency, community, humanity**
5	Number of years in existence	Number of years in its present form
6	Geographical presence	One site, multisites, multicities, multiple states, international
7	Description of operations	Text describing the basic operational activity of the organization; should relate closely to the mission statement

Nonprofit Spreadsheet.xls

ORG / GOV / REV / WRKFRC / COMP / EXMPT / NONEX / JOB

SPREADSHEET 2   ABC COMMUNITY
                 SERVICES–GOVERNANCE

Mission Statement: Provide Service to Those in Need

	A	B
		Nonprofit Spreadsheet.xls
1		Governance
2	Governing board	Name
3	Number of members	#
4	Board member finances	Y/N
5	Elected/Appointed officials	Y/N
6	Board member titles	List
7	Ex officio members:	
8	Number:	
9	Titles:	
10	Terms of service	Number of years, staggered terms (Y/N)
11	Quorum for decisions	Required attendance (percent/number/specific board members)
12	Number of meetings per year	Number and schedule
13	Role of governing body:	
14	Conduct fundraising	Y/N
15	Conduct budget request and negotiations	Y/N
16	Approve salary increase budget	Y/N
17	Approve changes to compensation structure	Y/N
18	Approve CEO/Executive director salary	Y/N
19	Approve top management salaries	Y/N
20	Approve other salaries	Y/N
21	Approve (some) new hires	Y/N
22	Other	Describe

ORG \ **GOV** \ REV \ WRKFRC \ COMP \ EXMPT \ NONEX \ JOB

SPREADSHEET 3   ABC COMMUNITY SERVICES—
REVENUE

Mission Statement: Provide Service to Those in Need

	A	B
		Nonprofit Spreadsheet.xls
1	Fund sources	List names, amounts, and percents
2	Annual budget cycle	Y/N - describe
3	Formal budget request process	Y/N - describe
4	Required reporting:	Y/N - describe
5	Government contracts	Y/N - describe
6	Other required reporting	Y/N - describe
7	Fund accounting	Y/N - describe
8	Fundraising	Y/N - describe
9	Donors	Y/N - describe
10	Government support	Y/N - describe
11	Budget based on revenue predictions	Y/N - describe
12	Voter influence	Y/N - describe

ORG / GOV \ **REV** / WRKFRC / COMP / EXMPT / NONEX / JOB

Legend:

Fund Sources: List each fund source in the previous fiscal year with each respective total annual dollar amount and percentage of total funding.

Annual Budget Cycle: The timing of budget activity, lines of authority for approvals, degree of detail.

Formal Budget Request Process: Is there a formal or informal process through which the organization obtains its budget for the coming fiscal year? If so, describe its timeframe, administrative burden, and other aspects.

Required Reporting: Does the organization have to file reports for government(s) based on the type(s) of funding it receives? If so, what types of reports, how often, and degree of administrative burden? Does the organization have to file reports to nongovernment entities based on the type(s) of funding it receives? If so, what types of reports, how often, and degree of administrative burden?

Fund Accounting: Does the organization use this type of accounting to track the use of each dollar of funding received into the organization?

Fundraising: A formal or informal and coordinated effort, routine or ad hoc, to persuade individuals outside the organization to donate funds. Describe the administrative burden, percent of budget obtained through this process, and any other aspects of fundraising.

Donors: Individuals outside the organization who have donated funds to it, currently or in the past, or might donate in the future. There may be significant administrative activity around these individuals.

Government Support: What sort of governmental influence impacts the organization including funding, regulatory control, budget approval, voter influence, or other?

Budget Based on Revenue Predictions: What are the predictive methods and algorithms used to forecast the budget for the coming year? Is revenue considered fixed or can the budget vary throughout the year?

Voter Influence: How can voters impact the organization?

SPREADSHEET 4   ABC COMMUNITY SERVICES—
THE WORKFORCE

Mission Statement: Provide Service to Those in Need

	A	B	C	D	E
1		Employee Group	Number Full-Time	Number Part-Time	Number Variable-Time
2		Senior management: M			
3		F			
4		Middle managment: M			
5		F			
6	Exempt	Professional: M			
7		F			
8		Other exempt: M			
9		F			
10		Confidential: M			
11		F			
12		Administrative: M			
13		F			
14	Nonexempt	Skilled crafts: M			
15		F			
16		Laborers: M			
17		F			
18		Other: M			
19		F			

ORG / GOV / REV / WRKFRC / COMP / EXMPT / NONEX / JOBS / NewCOMP / PerfMgt / MAINT

Legend:

Employee Group: Broad groupings of employees based on jobs of similar type and scope. M and F are male and female. Include any other useful demographic categories.

Number Full-Time: Number of full-time employees.

Number Part-Time: Number of part-time employees.

Number Variable-Time: Number of variable-time employees.

Appointment Terms: Employment contract, at will, represented, and other terms applicable to employees in this group.

F	G	H	I	J
Appointment Terms	Unionized	Average Years of Service	Average Age	Average Salary
	N/A			
	N/A			
	N/A			
	N/A			
	N/A			
	Y/N			
	Y/N			
	Y/N			
	Y/N			

Unionized: Group is represented by a collective bargaining unit.

Average Years of Service: Average number of years with the organization for members of this group.

Average Age: The average age of employees in this group.

Average Salary: Average base salary for employees in this group.

SPREADSHEET 5 ABC COMMUNITY SERVICES—CURRENT COMPENSATION

Mission Statement: Provide Service to Those in Need

Nonprofit Spreadsheet.xls

	A	B	C	D	E	F
1		**Employee Group**	**Number**	**Unionized**	**Average Years in Job**	**Pay Structure**
2	Exempt	Senior management		N/A		
3	Exempt	Middle management		N/A		
4	Exempt	Professional		N/A		
5	Exempt	Other exempt		N/A		
6	Exempt	Confidential		N/A		
7	Nonexempt	Administrative		Y/N		
8	Nonexempt	Skilled crafts		Y/N		
9	Nonexempt	Laborers		Y/N		
10	Nonexempt	Other		Y/N		

ORG / GOV / REV / WRKFRC / **COMP** / EXMPT / NONEX / JOBS / NewCOMP / PerfMgt / MAINT

Are any or all of the following in place: an organization chart, payroll/HRIS, central HR files on all employees?

Legend:

Employee Group: Broad groupings of employees based on jobs of similar type and scope. This column should begin with the same employee groups found on the WRKFRC spreadsheet and include M, F, and EEO categories if the WRKFRC spreadsheet indicates potential EEO issues.

Number: Number of employees in this group or subgroup.

Unionized: Members of this group or subgroup represented by a collective bargaining unit.

Average Years in Job: The average number of years served in the job currently held by members of this group or subgroup.

Pay Structure: Individual negotiation, ranges, flat rate, other.

Job Descriptions: Yes (available for all employees in group), no (for no employees in group), some (only for some of the employees in the group).

G	H	I	J	K
Job Descriptions	Salaries Public	Performance Management	Salary Increase Date	Compensation Authority

Salaries Public: Are salaries for jobs in this group available to the general public? To the employee population?

Performance Management: Is there a performance management process in place for all/some/none of the employees in this group?

Salary Increase Date: When do employees in this group become eligible for base salary increases? (Common date? Anniversary? Other?)

Compensation Authority: Describe the authority level(s) for approving compensation arrangements for members of the group.

SPREADSHEET 6   ABC COMMUNITY SERVICES—
THE EXEMPT WORKFORCE

Mission Statement: Provide Service to Those in Need

	A	B	C	D	E
	Employee Group	Jobs	Revenue Impact	Base Pay	Base Pay Increases
1					
2	Senior management	Job 1			
3		Job 2			
4	Middle management	Job 1			
5		Job 2			
6	Professional	Job 1			
7		Job 2			
8	Other exempt	Job 1			
9		Job 2			
10	Confidential	Job 1			
11		Job 2			

ORG / GOV / REV / WRKFRC / COMP \ EXMPT / NONEX / JOBS / NewCOMP / PerfMgt / MAINT /

Legend:

Employee Group: Broad groupings of employees based on jobs of similar type and scope. Because this spreadsheet may become extensive, the compensation manager may wish to omit EEO categories unless previous spreadsheets have indicated that serious issues need to be explored. For simplicity, this spreadsheet does not display EEO categories.

Jobs: A set of duties to be performed by one or more incumbents. The job may be vacant but under recruitment.

Revenue Impact: How does performance in the job affect revenue?

Base Pay: Set according to pay ranges, individual negotiation, union contract, flat rate, other?

Base Pay Increase: Based on merit, seniority, longevity, COLA, general increase, other?

Variable Pay	Person-Based Pay	Health Benefits	Pension / Retirement	Perquisites	Compensation Authority

Variable Pay: Based on individual, team-based, organization-wide performance.

Person-Based Pay: Based on competency, knowledge, skill, other.

Health Benefits: List.

Pension/Retirement: List types such as 403(b), 457, defined benefit, defined contribution.

Perquisites: Could the organization elect to give one or more employees in this job a perquisite? Does the organization currently do so? If so, what types of perquisites? Are any perquisites explicitly forbidden?

Compensation Authority: Describe the authority level(s) for approving compensation arrangements for jobs in this group.

SPREADSHEET 7   ABC COMMUNITY SERVICES—
THE NONEXEMPT WORKFORCE

Mission Statement: Provide Service to Those in Need

	A	B	C	D	E
1	Employee Group	Jobs	Revenue Impact	Base Pay	Base Pay Increase
2	Administrative	Job A			
3		Job B			
4	Skilled crafts	Job A			
5		Job B			
6	Laborers	Job A			
7		Job B			
8	Other unionized	Job A			
9		Job B			

Tabs: ORG / GOV / REV / WRKFRC / COMP / EXMPT / **NONEX** / JOBS / NewCOMP / PerfMgt / MAINT

Legend:

Employee Group: Broad groupings of employees based on Jobs of similar type and scope. Because this spreadsheet may become extensive, the compensation manager may wish to omit EEO categories unless previous spreadsheets have indicated that serious issues need to be explored.

Job: A set of duties, or job, held by one or more employees or vacant but under recruitment.

Revenue Impact: How does performance in the Job affect revenue?

Base Pay: Set according to pay ranges, individual negotiation, union contract, flat rate, other?

Base Pay Increase: Based on merit, seniority, longevity, COLA, general increase, other?

Variable Pay: Based on performance as an individual, team member, organization member.

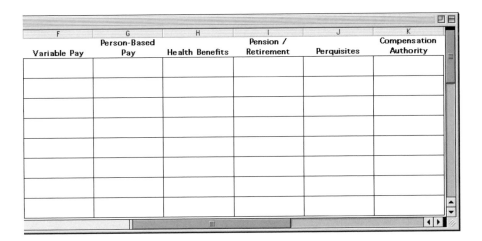

Variable Pay	Person-Based Pay	Health Benefits	Pension / Retirement	Perquisites	Compensation Authority

Person-Based: Competency, knowledge, skill.

Health Benefits: List.

Pension/Retirement: List type(s), such as 403(b), 457, defined benefit, defined contributions, and so on.

Perquisites: Could the organization elect to give one or more employees in this Job a perquisite? Does the organization currently do so? If so, what types of perquisites? Are any perquisites explicitly forbidden?

Compensation Authority: Describe the authority level(s) for approving compensation arrangements for Jobs in this group.

SPREADSHEET 8   ABC COMMUNITY SERVICES— THE JOBS

Mission Statement: Provide Service to Those in Need

	Nonprofit Spreadsheet.xls					
	A	B	C	D	E	F	G

	Employee Group	Jobs	Number of Incumbents	Revenue Impact	Job Analysis	
					Job Description	Job Specifications
Senior management	Job 1					
	Job 2					
Middle management	Job 1					
	Job 2					
Professional	Job 1					
	Job 2					
Other exempt	Job 1					
	Job 2					
Confidential	Job 1					
	Job 2					
Administrative	Job A					
	Job B					
Skilled crafts	Job A					
	Job B					
Laborers	Job A					
	Job B					
Other unionized	Job A					
	Job B					

Tabs: ORG / GOV / REV / WRKFRC / COMP / EXMPT / NONEX \ JOBS / NewCOMP / PerfMgt / MAINT /

Legend:

Employee Group: Broad groupings of employees based on jobs of similar type and scope. This column should begin with the same employee groups found on the WRKFRC spreadsheet and include M, F, and EEO categories if the WRKFRC spreadsheet indicates potential EEO issues.

Job: A set of duties, or job, held by one or more employees or vacant but under recruitment.

Number of Incumbents: The number of employees who hold this job.

Revenue Impact: How does performance in the job affect revenue?

Job Description: A summary of a job's purpose and its tasks, duties, and responsibilities.

Job Specifications: Skills, knowledge, and abilities required for the job.

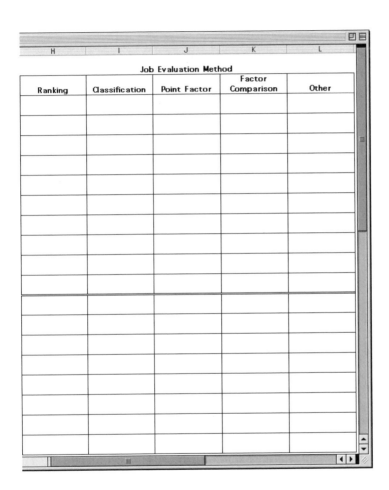

H	I	J	K	L
		Job Evaluation Method		
Ranking	Classification	Point Factor	Factor Comparison	Other

Ranking: A collection of job content evaluation techniques that compare jobs with each other or against general criteria.

Classification: A whole job evaluation technique that places jobs into grades or classifications on the basis of at least one benchmark job per grade.

Point Method: A quantitative job evaluation technique assigning points to compensable factors that describe jobs.

Factor Comparison: Selection of compensable factors for each job, then ranking all jobs by factor.

Other: For example, slotting.

SPREADSHEET 9   ABC COMMUNITY SERVICES—
NEW COMPENSATION STRUCTURE

Mission Statement: Provide Service to Those in Need

	A	B	C	D	E	F	G	H	I
1						New Salary Range			
2		Range Code	Employee Group	Jobs	Minimum	Middle	Maximum	Spread Percent	Steps
3			Senior management	Job 1					
4				Job 2					
5			Middle management	Job 1					
6				Job 2					
7	Exempt		Professional	Job 1					
8				Job 2					
9			Other exempt	Job 1					
10				Job 2					
11			Confidential	Job 1					
12				Job 2					
13			Administrative	Job A					
14				Job B					
15	Nonexempt		Skilled crafts	Job A					
16				Job B					
17			Laborers	Job A					
18				Job B					
19			Other unionized	Job A					
20				Job B					

Tabs: ORG / GOV / REV / WRKFRC / COMP / EXMPT / NONEX / JOBS / NewCOMP / PerfMgt / MAINT

Legend:

Range Code: A code identifying the salary range that sets the minimum and maximum salary rates for jobs within the range.

Employee Group: Broad groupings of employees based on jobs of similar type and scope. This column reflects any revisions to the employee groups, including revisions intended to address any EEO issues, and the employee groups shown here may differ from the employee groups shown on the WRKFRC and other previous spreadsheets.

Jobs: A set of duties performed by one or more incumbents. The job may be vacant but under recruitment.

New Salary Range: The minimum, midpoint, and maximum salary levels for a new salary range. If blank or 0, this particular job is not compensated according to a salary range.

Spread Percent: The difference between the maximum and minimum rates divided by the minimum rate and expressed as a percentage.

Steps: The number of steps in the range. A blank or 0 entry would indicate that there are no steps.

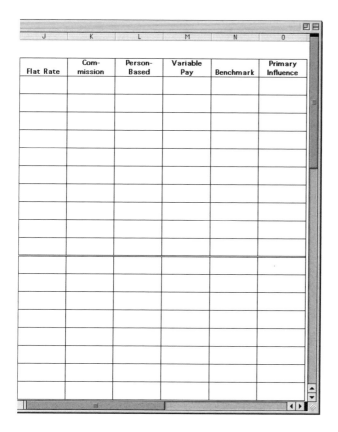

Flat Rate: A single hourly rate at which all incumbents in the job are paid. If the rate is other than hourly, the column should show the rate and the applicable time period, for example, monthly, annual, other.

Commission: An arrangement by which incumbents in the job receive some portion of the revenue attributed to their efforts.

Person-Based Pay: Pay based on skills, knowledge, and/or competency acquired by the incumbents in this job.

Variable Pay: The basis of any variable pay that may be earned by incumbents in this job—for example, individual, team-based, or organizational.

Benchmark: The relationship of this job to the external labor market, either as a benchmark or linked to another job used as a benchmark.

Primary Influence: The entity, statistic, mechanism, comparison, or other influence that has the dominant effect on compensation for this job.

SPREADSHEET 10   ABC COMMUNITY SERVICES—
PERFORMANCE MANAGEMENT

Mission Statement: Provide Service to Those in Need

	Employee Group	Jobs	Revenue Impact	Performance Review Schedule	Salary Increase Schedule
1					
2	Senior management	Job 1			
3		Job 2			
4	Middle management	Job 1			
5		Job 2			
6	Professional	Job 1			
7		Job 2			
8	Other exempt	Job 1			
9		Job 2			
10	Confidential	Job 1			
11		Job 2			
12	Administrative	Job A			
13		Job B			
14	Skilled crafts	Job A			
15		Job B			
16	Laborers	Job A			
17		Job B			
18	Other unionized	Job A			
19		Job B			

(Rows 2–11 grouped as **Exempt**; rows 12–19 grouped as **Nonexempt**. Workbook title: Nonprofit Spreadsheet.xls. Sheet tabs: ORG / GOV / REV / WRKFRC / COMP / EXMPT / NONEX / JOBS / NewCOMP / **PerfMgt** / MAINT)

Legend:

Employee Group: Broad groupings of employees based on jobs of similar type and scope. This column reflects any revisions to the employee groups, including revisions intended to address any EEO issues, and the employee groups shown here may differ from the employee groups shown on the WRKFRC and other previous spreadsheets.

Jobs: A set of duties performed by one or more incumbents. The job may be vacant but under recruitment.

Revenue Impact: How does performance in the job affect revenue?

Performance Review Schedule: The timing of performance reviews for incumbent(s) in the job.

Salary Increase Schedule: The timing of the effective date of salary increases for incumbents in the job.

Compensation Arrangement: The nature of the compensation applicable to this job under the new structure, for example, ranges with or without steps, flat rates, commissions, variable pay, other.

Base Salary Increase: The relationship between base salary increases and the performance management process.

Variable Pay: Type(s) of variable pay for which incumbent(s) in the job are eligible.

Measurement Basis: Performer-oriented, behavior-oriented, results-oriented, comparison-oriented, other.

Performance Review Technique: List the performance review technique(s) for the job such as BARS, graphic rating, essay, 360-degree, other.

SPREADSHEET 11   ABC COMMUNITY SERVICES—
MAINTAINING THE STRUCTURE

Mission Statement: Provide Service to Those in Need

	A	B	C	D	E
		Employee Group	Jobs	Status	Job Description
1					
2	Exempt	Senior management	Job 1		
3			Job 2		
4		Middle management	Job 1		
5			Job 2		
6		Professional	Job 1		
7			Job 2		
8		Other exempt	Job 1		
9			Job 2		
10		Confidential	Job 1		
11			Job 2		
12	Nonexempt	Administrative	Job A		
13			Job B		
14		Skilled crafts	Job A		
15			Job B		
16		Laborers	Job A		
17			Job B		
18		Other unionized	Job A		
19			Job B		

Nonprofit Spreadsheet.xls

ORG / GOV / REV / WRKFRC / COMP / EXMPT / NONEX / JOBS / NewCOMP / PerfMgt \ MAINT /

Legend:

Employee Group: Broad groupings of employees based on jobs of similar type and scope. Any changes to the employee groups themselves as a result of structure maintenance would be shown in this column. Such changes are likely to be linked to other more general human resources changes.

Jobs: A set of duties performed by one or more incumbents. The job may be vacant but under recruitment.

Status: Is this job under revision, to be added, to be deleted, or in some other status?

Job Description: Does the job description for the job exist (if new) or need to be revised?

Job Evaluation: Does the job need to be reevaluated according to the selected job evaluation technique?

Job Evaluation	Turnover	Compensation Arrangement	Impact	Management View

Turnover: Recruitment/retention statistics for the Job.

Compensation Arrangement: Is the compensation arrangement for the position changed as part of the maintenance effort and, if so, what is the new arrangement?

Impact: The automated systems and organizational units, including labor unions, that will be affected by the revision, if any, to this job.

Management View: Formal or informal feedback from management and/or the governing body regarding the job, the employee group, or the structure itself.

HRIS Data Elements

The following data elements and their respective definitions evolved over five years of class assignments. Beginning with a minimal set of data elements in 1999, each successive class has added HRIS data elements or revised definitions as part of a class project. The list reflects the accumulation of this student-contributed HRIS information through summer 2004. (Most of these students are Human Resources practitioners.)

Students perceived the first set of data elements as "person-related," addressing the employee as a person rather than the holder of a specific job.

The second set of data elements is position-related and could conceivably apply to an employee who has two separate (and probably part-time) jobs for the same employer, a situation that can occur in higher education institutions as well as others.

The remaining sets of data elements deal with training and development, recruiting, and applicant tracking.

PERSON-RELATED

Data	*Purpose/Type of Information*
Access to alarm system	Y/N, code assigned to employee
Achievements	Special accomplishments
Applicant for internal position	What position and when
Automobile allowance	Amount
Awards/bonuses	Dollar amount
Beneficiary information	Fields as required for each benefit program
Benefits	One field for each benefit program
Benefits expiration date	DD/MM/YYYY
Benefits > $50K	Income tax trigger
Birthdate	Demographic studies, celebrations
Car cleaning services—mobile	Optional deduction
Car license number(s)	For emergency evacuation purposes
Citizenship	Allows selection of foreign nationals
Claim	Date filed, expected date of return, type of claim
COBRA eligibility	Y/N, code for qualifying event
Commission date	Date when commissions must be paid to employee
Community service	Text or code indicating type of service
Complaint(s) against . . .	Record of complaints against employee from external sources
Computer literacy	Y/N field or could be a code showing degree of proficiency
Concierge	Optional deduction
Court orders	Regarding appearance dates, etc.
Court sanction(s)	Date(s) amount(s)

Data	Purpose/Type of Information
CPR training	Y/N, possibly date
Credit cards	Cards (type, number, expiration date) issued by employer to employee
Criminal background	Background check, felony box on application, and so on
Current status	Active, on leave, separated, retired, dead
Damages for a person	Amount
Dependents	Benefits including COBRA, retirement
Disability insurance	State, waiting period, known prior claims
Disability status	American Disabilities Act, type
Discipline	Primary background/education discipline
DL classification	Type of vehicle
DL number	Additional identification, driving company vehicles
DMV number	Driver's license number (a public and unique identifier)
Driver's auto insurance renewal	Y/N, MM/DD/YYYY
Driver's license renewal	Date on which it should be renewed
Driving record	DMV-based record of violations
Drug tests	Y/N, type, employment outcome
Dry cleaning services	Optional deduction
Education	Earned degree level; major/minor; additional classes and certificates, institution where earned
Elected options	One field for each benefit program
E-mail address	Contact employee in an official way but less than correspondence
Emergency information	Provide assistance to employee in case of accident or other harm
Employee number/ payroll number	Employer-generated unique identifier

Data	*Purpose/Type of Information*
Employee-paid premium cost	Cost per pay period
Employee physical information	A set of fields including date of physical, results, required vaccinations
Equipment issued	A recurring field itemizing each piece of equipment issued to employee along with serial numbers, if appropriate
Ethnic identity	Demographic studies, affirmative action, EEO
Events attendance	Number of special events attended divided by number of events hosted by employer
Exit interview results	Code indicating whether interview took place and, if so, content
Experience	Related to skills
FACIS test result	Code indicating test result
Fax number	Nearest fax machine to employee
Fingerprint	Y/N field if company has fingerprinted employee
First aid training	Date
First name	Identifier
Garnishments	Code to indicate reason(s) for garnishments
Gender	Demographic studies, affirmative action, EEO, transgender status
Grants/research/ publications	All indications of research activity
Handbook review (annual)	Y/N, date
Hire date—earliest	Seniority calculations, annual evaluation date
Hire date(s)—subsequent	Date(s) used to calculate breaks in service affecting seniority

Data	*Purpose/Type of Information*
Home address	Company correspondence, zip code kept separate, W-2s, separation documents, retirement payments
I-9 status	Proof that employee can work in United States; type of proof; documents provided, expiration date
Key to building(s)	Y/N, which buildings if a large site
Languages	Recurring field, one for each language
Last day on pay status	Separation agreements, inquiries, related payments
Last day worked	Separation agreements, related payments
Last employer	Employer prior to initial hire
Leave begin date	MM/DD/YYYY
Leave certification code/data	FMLA (Family Medical Leave Act), medical, personal, military/reserve, FFLA (Family Friendly Leave Act)
Leave end date	MM/DD/YYYY
Leave status	On leave Y/N
Legal services—prepaid	Optional deduction
Length of service	Dates, types
License/certificate renewal dates	Must renew licenses or certificates or can no longer practice specialties
Licenses/certificates	Legally allowed to practice certain specialties
Long-term disability	Through employer
Maiden name	Whether currently used
Mailing address	Address to which company correspondence must be sent
Marital status	Benefits including COBRA, retirement
Meal reduction	Amount

Data	*Purpose / Type of Information*
Medical flag	Condition that could require employer intervention in the workplace (Y/N)
Middle initial/middle name	Allows further identification refinement, for example, "John Q. Smith"
Military discharge	Type
Military status	Code showing previous military experience, veteran status, reserve affiliation
Money banks	For cashier responsibilities
Name—last	Legal last name, additional last name(s)
Name—qualifier of last	Includes "Jr.," "Sr.," II, III, etc.
Next performance review date	Triggers managers to prepare for reviews
Ninety-day probation/ introductory period	Date when the 90-day probationary period is up
Notary public	Y/N field to indicate if qualified as Notary Public
Orientation—general	Date employee attended employer's orientation session (MM/DD/YYYY)
Orientation—safety	Date employee attended employer's safety in workplace orientation session (MM/DD/YYYY)
Other names/aliases	Allows for artistic names, DBAs (Doing Business As), and so forth
Pager number	To reach employee "on call" or during normal work day
Parking sticker	Code or number depending on how employer handles parking designations
Paycheck distribution	A "snapshot" of the deductions to better answer employee questions
Paycheck distribution election	Direct deposit, company delivery, mail to home, or other

Data	*Purpose/Type of Information*
Personnel program	Employee category (if applicable), contract, at will
Phone number—cell	Company supplied phones—related inventory and contact
Phone number—home	Alternate phone number where employee may be reached or message may be left
Phone number—work extension	3 or 4 digits, usually
Physical examination (corp.)	Y/N, date keyed, date of birth
Photograph	Employee picture, possible in recent technology
Policy manual acknowledgment	Y/N, date. This could be a multiple field with separate entries for each type of policy acknowledgment (harassment, at will, HIPAA, etc.)
Pretax deductions	401K and other deductions from the gross pay
Previous addresses	Can go back as far as 5 years
Previous last name	Maiden name, former name, used for employee history
Prior service	With state, with this employer, with some other employer
Professional associations	Memberships: employer-paid, employee-paid, honorary, others
Professional development	Activities of involvement
Recreation privilege	Gym, recreation facility, other
Rehire eligibility	Code indicating Y or N
Religious preference	Type
Retirement status	Coverage by company retirement program(s), vested Y/N
Salary (total) change history	Salary increases/decreases over time

Data	*Purpose/Type of Information*
Security clearance	Federal requirements; company classification
Seniority	Years with the company including breaks in service; service credit
Separation date	Date employer and employee "agree" that separation will take place
Separation reason	The nature of the separation: resignation, layoff, termination for cause, retirement
Sexual harassment training	Y/N, date
Safety shoes	Amount; through payroll deduction
Sick leave accrual rate	Earned per period
Sick leave balance	Abuse of sick leave; separation
Signing documents (annual)	Y/N, date, can include confidentiality/ arbitration
Skills	Internal promotion efforts
Social security number	Government-generated unique identifier
Short-term disability	Through employer
Subordinate relationship	Difficulties with subordinates, complaints, secretary retention record
Supplementary retirement contribution	Amount to be taken from employee's paycheck to go into retirement fund
Supplementary retirement	Participation in supplementary retirement plans (401k, 403b, stock options, other)
Tardiness	Number of occurrences and dates
Tax exemptions	Paycheck calculations
Travel profile	Preferences with respect to airlines, hotels, other
Trial record	Number of trials won, number of trials lost
Tuition reimbursement	Amount, date check was written
Union membership	Applicable contract

Data	*Purpose/Type of Information*
Uniform allowance	Amount; type
Vacation leave allowed and taken	Running leave balances
Vacation leave accrual	As a person, can have two jobs with different accrual rates
Veteran status	Demographics; protected class; cross-reference to disability
Workers compensation code	Category according to workers' compensation regulations

POSITION-RELATED

Data	*Purpose/Type of Information*
Actual annualized rate	Annualized Rate × Percent of Time
Actual monthly earnings	Base + Ancillary. Used for workers' comp or disability
Administrative stipend	A sum paid to an employee to assume administrative responsibilities in addition to existing duties.
Annualized rate	Derived if not basic
Applicable ancillary pay	O/T, call back, on call, shift differentials, hazardous pay, other occasional special rates.
At will employee	Process completed including employee notification and acknowledgement
Base salary rate	Hourly, monthly, biweekly, bimonthly, or annual
Benefits eligibility	As a result of this position; P/T, F/T
Benefits eligibility date	MM/DD/YYYY
Benefits waiting period	Number of days
Bonding/security clearance	A formal testimony that the employee is innocent of certain actions and therefore worthy of trust
Budget expense group	The organizational unit/division to which this employee's salary is charged
COBRA	Initial notification date, notification date, qualifying event
Collective bargaining	Position is covered by union contract or rate follows positions covered by union contract
Compa-ratio	Individual's salary divided by midpoint of the range for the position

Data	*Purpose/Type of Information*
Compensation arrangement	Eligibility for bonus, profit sharing, steps within a range, open range, fixed rate, collectively bargained arrangement, commission structure, and any other compensation arrangements that apply to this position and any other positions similarly defined
Confidential/ nonconfidential	Position would normally be covered by union contract but is not because of participation in management decisions.
Conflict of interest requirements	Certain positions may be prohibited or required to refrain from or participate in various kinds of transactions and reporting
Contract	Y/N; related information if Y
Corporate property	Car, laptop, phone, and so forth assigned to employee and in his/her possession off company property
Current leave balances	Vacation leave, sick leave, and any other type of leave such as paid time off
Department	Organizational unit to which position belongs
Duration of appointment— Change	Date and code showing previous appointment type
Duration of appointment— Type	Temporary, regular, other, seasonal
EEO Class	Reporting purposes
Eligible for reimbursement for travel expenses	Y/N, qualifying circumstances
Eligible for tuition reimbursement	Y/N; cap on total amount or amount per class, per year, job-related eligibility requirements

Data	Purpose/Type of Information
Employee relations code	Supervisor, confidential
Excused absences	FMLA, workers' comp, other
Executive benefits	Nonsalary benefits and perquisites to which incumbent is entitled
Exempt/Nonexempt	Eligibility for overtime, call back, on call, shift differentials, and other ancillary pay (separate fields for each)
Hobbies	Text
Hours on pay status	In previous period
Hours worked	In previous period
Job description on file	Y/N
Job title	Describes work performed, personnel program membership, and place in organization
Leave accrual date	Date leave accrual rate changes; type of leave
Name—referral	Name of the individual who referred the employee for the position
Next performance review date	Date on which the employee should receive an assessment of his/her performance in this job
Next salary review date	Date on which the employee should receive notification of his/her pay change, if any
Outcome of last review(s)	The rating or score given to the employee at his/her *prior* review(s)
Overtime requirements	Amount and type of overtime required for the position
Pay frequency	Monthly, semimonthly, biweekly, weekly
Pay grade range	Minimum, maximum, midpoint
Pay grades	Civil service-type system or employer created

Data	Purpose/Type of Information
Percent of time/FTE	Expected time on job or work schedule/full-time equivalent
Percentage increase in pay	Percentage increases in salary, by period, over time
Percentage of time	Indication of the degree of part-time employment in the position
Personnel program	The program policies governing the terms and conditions of appointment for the position
Physical restriction	Code showing type of restriction
Position control number	Budget control
Position history	Titles used in past and related dates; changes in FLSA status, replacement or new position, other
Previous salary history	Salary at employer prior to initial hire
Primary department	The department handling the administrative transactions regarding the employee who holds more than one appointment in more than one department
Probationary status	Y/N; related information
Promotion review date	The number of days after promotion when review has taken/will take place
Rate class	A field that tells whether rate is determined by a memorandum of understanding, the human resources office, or other
Relocation eligibility	Y/N
Required degree	Degree(s) or professional designation(s) required for the position
Reports to	Title of supervisor/manager who directly reviews employee performance
Review—date of last	Date the employee was given a performance evaluation
Review—date of next	MM/DD/YYYY

Data	*Purpose/Type of Information*
Safety equipment	Recurring field for each safety item required by the job
Safety training	Required training for the position: type, timing, completion
Salary increase—date of last	MM/DD/YYYY; salary history
Salary increase manager	Manager who determines salary increases for employees in a group of positions
Shift	First/second/third and differential, if any
Sick leave balance	Balance based on accrual for this position. Useful if employee holds more than one position and each position entails different accrual rates
Site/location	Place where work is performed
Skills/licenses	Identify job-required licenses, certifications, and other formal requirements
Software requirements	Types of software employee must know and use in the position
Tardies	Number of times in appropriate period that employee was late to work
Tier	A number—for example, I, II—which denotes a category of position that shares certain terms and conditions of appointments with other positions in that tier
Title/job code	A set of digits associated uniquely with a particular job title
Training received	Classes completed
Training requirements	Y/N; type, time when required (after six months, one year, etc.)
Transfer info	Date and origin of transfer from within employer
Travel required	Anyone in this position must travel

Data	*Purpose/Type of Information*
Turnover related to this position	Number of separations per year
Unexcused absences	Number of occurrences; number of days
Uniform required	Y/N
Vacation leave accrual rate	Rate of vacation leave accrual per period for this position, maximum accrual, cash-out option
Vacation leave balance	Number of days of earned vacation not yet taken
Work environmental requirements	Hazardous duty, exceptional hours, and so forth
Work week—change	Full-time to part-time or the reverse
Work week—standard	Number of hours, specific days, shifts
Workers' Compensation classification	Code indicating classification and rate

ADDITIONAL BENEFITS INFORMATION

- Terms of each contract → benefits threshold level
- End date of each contract with benefit provider
- Actuarial assumptions
- Employee demographics

Terms of the contract may allow employers to control benefits eligibility by controlling percentage of time to control, for example, 30 hours threshold for employee participation.

The contract end date alerts HR when benefits will be renegotiated. Prior to the negotiation process, the HR director of compensation/benefits manager will want to know the pattern of employee usage of the benefits options provided by the current contract(s). Options not selected by employees could be bargaining points for lower premiums in the next contract.

TRAINING AND DEVELOPMENT

Data	*Purpose/Type of Information*
Accrued training costs for this employee	Amount (accrued as of date of this report)
Authorizing manager	Name
Continuing education program	Type of program
Continuing education cost	Employer costs
Contribution to employer as a result of training	Can be amount, code, or text
Customer evaluation	Rating by customer of employee
Department number requesting training	The code identifying the department
Employee conduct during training	Attendance; class participation
Employee goal/intended result	The desired outcome of the training according to the employee or according to the employer
Employee's most recent performance date	MM/DD/YYYY
Employee's rating	Employee's rating of this training experience
Funding source	Account or fund appropriate to organization
Hours of training	Total accumulated
Intended result	Certification, license, degree, competence level
Manager's rating	Manager's rating of this training experience
Name	Employee who received the training
Performance rating after training	Coded 1–5

Data	*Purpose/Type of Information*
Performance rating before training	Coded 1–5
Required training classes	Name, date, why required
Salary before training	Amount/month or hour or year
Salary increase after training	Percentage and amount
Session cost to employee	Amount
Success index	A single number comprising salary increase, performance change, manager's assessment, and employee's assessment
Succession rating	Likelihood of promotion; type of career path
Trainer	External, internal, other
Training history	Classes taken and when, results
Training points total—current	Summary of number of classes, number of occurrences, or other statistics selected by employer
Training priority	A code indicating such priorities as immediate performance, legal requirement, or future project
Training site	Company premises, hotel, training center, other
Travel expense	Employer-paid
Turnover learning curve	Time to complete mastery of area
Type of training	Subject matter, probably coded (discipline or skill), mentoring formal or informal, books read

RECRUITMENT

Data	*Purpose/Type of Information*
Accrued cost this fiscal year	Amount paid to this outreach organization/person
Ad placement and date	Multiple occurrences
Ad text	The full text of a posting on any media
Additional services provided	Other client services in addition to recruitment
Applicant count	Number of applicants received in current year from this source
Competitor marketing	Contacting employees at competitor organizations, that is, raiding
Contact person	Individual or Web address
Cost of ad placement	Amount
Fee structure	Flat fee, per placement, other
Financial arrangement	On account, per occurrence, other
Internal/external	Whether the position is to be filled from the inside or externally, either by intent or by circumstance
Interview method	Type of technique (structured, behavioral, other) used to interview
New hire count	Number of applicants hired in current year from this source
Phone/fax/e-mail	Communication
Position description	Set of responsibilities and minimum qualifications for the position
Qualified applicant count	The number of applicants received in current year from this recruitment source who met minimum qualifications
Rating	A code indicating actual results from this source

Data	*Purpose/Type of Information*
Reason for opening	A code indicating whether the position is new or existing and reason why vacated
Recruiter address	Mailing/street address of recruiter
Recruitment name	Name of organization/person publicizing position
Recruitment specialty	Engineering, info systems, office personnel, general, exec, other
Recruitment type	Newspaper, professional association, Internet, search firm, temp agency, other
Recruitment/contract terms	Temp to perm, exclusive, and so forth
Requisition longevity	Length of time requisition is active
School(s) recruited	Colleges/universities visited by recruitment agency
Selection experience	Whether the applicant was selected for interview, offer, hire
Submission procedure	Method by which positions under recruitment are communicated to outreach organization/person

APPLICANT TRACKING

Data	*Purpose/Type of Information*
Applicant name	Identification
Applicant number	Identification and an automatic count of number of applicants for this position.
Applicant's status	Internal, external, employed, new to area, related to existing employee, other, still under consideration; awaiting results of a related recruitment
Approval	Name/title of person approving the position
Assessment test(s)	Type, scores
Availability for work	When applicant can begin: week times, hours
Background status	Background check (Y/N); results; date of background check
Budget exception	Y/N; exception to standard terms and conditions for position
Contact information	Name(s), address(es), phone number(s), of individuals to be contacted regarding the applicant
Date of interview	Per occurrence
Date of resume	Date resume received. Tracks the recruitment process for this position and if resumes are put in a data base, indicates purge date.
Date position filled	MM/DD/YYYY successful applicant accepted the position
Date position open	MM/DD/YYYY
Date position requested	MM/DD/YYYY department formally requested the position
Degree and discipline	Experience and education

Data	*Purpose / Type of Information*
Designated successor	Determined to fill the position while still in another position
Disposition	Code showing that person was hired or the nonhire reason
Ethnic identity	Includes gender. Used for diversity and affirmative action reporting
Experience beyond	Experience possessed by the applicant in addition to the experience required by the position
Finder's fee	Y/N, if Y, to whom
Gender	M/F/T (Male, female, and transgender, which refers to individuals who are in the waiting period for a gender change operation.)
Geographic base	The size of the region from which applicants were recruited, for example, national, city, state, other
Hired	Y/N
Interview history	How many, with whom (name and title), other
Job skills	Skills, knowledge, and abilities possessed by the applicant and required by the position
Languages	If English not the native tongue, all other languages (speak, read, write)
Met min qualifications	Y/N
Offer amount	Amount in dollars
Offer made	Y/N, acceptance/rejection code, date
Orientation date	MM/DD/YYYY: anticipated orientation date for new hire

Data	*Purpose/Type of Information*
Package particulars	Those elements of the offer, such as relocation, housing allowance, and so forth
Position ID	Position for which applicant applied
Previous applicant	Whether applicant has applied before, dates
Previous competitor	Competing organization previously (or currently) employing the applicant
Previous employer	Identity of employer prior to applying for this position
Previous offer	Details regarding previous offer made to this applicant
Professional licenses/ certifications	Multiple occurrences
Rating on certification list	Where applicant ranks in comparison to other applicants for the position
Recruitment allowance	Money available to fill the position
Recruitment process	Hiring process for that position: selection committee, manager only, HR involvement, temp to perm, other
Recruitment source	Outreach name, friend, employee referral, other
Reference details	Comments made about employee
Referred by/to	Another department; employee
Referred to other jobs	Y/N; was this applicant referred for other jobs within the company?·
Rehire status	If formerly employed by this employer, eligible for rehire?
Relationships	Any relatives working for employer?
Relocation costs	Y/N—Origin
Requisition new/ replacement	N/R; indicates a position under repeated recruitment

Data	*Purpose/Type of Information*
Requesting department	Organizational unit supporting the position
Sell/serve alcohol	Whether the applicant is permitted by law to sell or to serve alcoholic beverages
Solicited	Y/N
Special accommodations	Type
Special skills	Sky diving, bull fighting, and so forth; multiple occurrences
Sponsorship	Y/N, country
Start date	MM/DD/YYYY
Testing advice	Advised of testing for drugs, physical abilities, other
Type of interview	First, second, HR, hiring manager, other (a code)
Volunteer or paid	Whether applicant requires compensation to work
Years' relevant experience	Number

Bibliography

"Broadbanding, Pay Ranges and Labor Costs," Charles Fay, PH.D., CCP; Eric Schulz; Steven E. Gross; and David Van De Voort, CCP, *WorldatWork Journal*, vol. 13, no. 2 (Second Quarter 2004), pp. 8–23.

Building a Fair Pay Program: A Step-by-Step Guide, 2nd edition, Roger J. Plachy and Sandra J. Plachy, New York: AMACOM (American Management Association), 1998.

Business-Driven Compensation Policies: Integrating Compensation Systems with Corporate Strategies, Robert L. Heneman, New York: AMACOM (American Management Association), 2001.

Compensation Decision Making, 4th Edition, Thomas J. Bergman and Vida Gulbinas Scarpello, Mason, OH: South-Western, Thomson Learning, 2002.

The Compensation Solution, John E. Tropman, San Francisco, CA: Jossey-Bass, 2001.

Designing Performance Appraisal Systems: Aligning Appraisals and Organizational Realities, Allan M. Mohrman, Jr., Susan M. Resnick-West, and Edward E. Lawler III, San Francisco, CA: Jossey-Bass, 1989.

"Fix Broken Performance Appraisal Systems," David P. Marino-Nachison, SHRM Home>Media HR Forum.

"Gainsharing and EVA: The U.S. Postal Service Experience," *WorldatWork Journal,* vol. 12, no. 1 (First Quarter 2003), pp. 21–30.

Human Resource Management, Robert L. Mathis and John H. Jackson, Mason, OH: South-Western, Thomson Learning, 2003.

Master File Key Element: Fund, University of Iowa Accounting Code Manual, available at *www.uiowa.edu/~fusas/accman/acmfund.htm* (5/29/2004).

Nonprofit Compensation and Benefits Practices, Carol L. Bareito and Jack P. Bowman, Hoboken, NJ: John Wiley & Sons, 1998.

Nonprofit Kit for Dummies, Stan Hutton and Frances Phillips, Hoboken, NJ: John Wiley & Sons, 2001.

Pay at Risk, John A. Turner, ed., Kalamazoo, MI: W.E. Upjohn Institute for Employment Research, 2001.

"Pay for Performance: From Theory to Reality," Dan Federman, *Workspan* (April 2004), pp. 42–44.

Pay People Right! Patricia K. Zingheim and Jay R. Schuster, San Francisco, CA: Jossey-Bass, 2000.

"Philanthropic Foundations Face Intense Pressures to Increase the Amount They Give to Charities," Ben Gose, *The Chronicle of Higher Education & The Chronicle of Philanthropy,* vol. 50, issue 38 (May 28, 2004), available at *http://chronicle.com/weekly/v50/i38/38b01201.htm.*

"Prudent Management or Outright Greed? Critics Ask How Big Endowments Should Be," Ben Gose, *The Chronicle of Higher Education & The Chronicle of Philanthropy,* Endowments (Special Supplement), vol. 50, issue 38 (May 28, 2004), available at *http://chronicle.com/weekly/v50/i38/38b00901.htm.*

Public Sector Compensation: An Overview of Present Practices and Emerging Trends, Howard Risher, PH.D. and Cary E. Randow, CCP, Scottsdale, AZ: American Compensation Association, 1998.

Rewarding Excellence: Pay Strategies for the New Economy, Edward E. Lawler III, San Francisco, CA: Jossey Bass, 2000.

The SHRM Learning System, Alexandria, VA: Society for Human Resource Management, 2004.

Strategic Compensation: A Human Resource Management Approach, Joseph J. Martocchio, Upper Saddle River, NJ: Prentice-Hall, 2001.

Index